A MORE PERFECT UNION

ALSO BY BEN CARSON, MD

WITH CANDY CARSON

One Nation
One Vote
America the Beautiful

WITH CECIL MURPHEY

Gifted Hands
Think Big

WITH GREGG LEWIS

Take the Risk
The Big Picture

WITH GREGG LEWIS AND DEBORAH SHAW LEWIS

You Have a Brain: A Teen's Guide to Think Big

A MORE PERFECT UNION

What We the People Can Do
to Protect Our Constitutional Liberties

BEN CARSON, MD,
with CANDY CARSON

Sentinel

SENTINEL
An imprint of Penguin Random House LLC
375 Hudson Street
New York, New York 10014
penguin.com

ISBN 978-1-59184-804-2

Printed in the United States of America
1   3   5   7   9   10   8   6   4   2

Set in Palatino LT Std Roman
Designed by Spring Hoteling

This book is dedicated to "we the people"
and the millions of people who sacrificed so much
in the past so that we could be free.

CONTENTS

CONTENTS

FOREWORD

AMBASSADOR C. BOYDEN GRAY

I first met Dr. Carson at my home during an event for the Carsons' Scholars Fund. One of the first things that struck me about him was his wide-ranging interests in fields unrelated to medicine. An expert in neurosurgery, he was not content to rest on his laurels. Instead, he surrounded himself with highly accomplished individuals from other fields and was eager to learn from them. Even more surprising, he already seemed to know quite a bit about the industries he was asking about.

As an ambassador, I have expertise in law and diplomacy, and it's rare to see someone who understands the challenges of government as well as Dr. Carson does. Though he has never held office, Dr. Carson has insight into the causes of our nation's problems that is keener than that of most elected officials'. He sees how essential a proper understanding of the Constitution is to America's freedom, and that's why I'm so excited to see this book.

Dr. Carson compellingly argues that every American should know what the Constitution actually says. The

American people's current lack of familiarity with our founding document is undermining our liberties, and Dr. Carson wants to stop the erosion before it is too late. Rather than waiting for someone else to act, he has provided an excellent primer to remedy this basic ignorance.

In this highly readable layman's introduction to the key elements of the Constitution, Dr. Carson explains why limited government and the separation of powers are necessary for the preservation of liberty. He offers a compelling explanation of the dangers of big government and the benefits of restraining it.

Dr. Carson's ability to weave in stories from his own extraordinary experience as one of the country's leading pediatric neurosurgeons makes *A More Perfect Union* all the more intriguing. His storytelling ability is one of the charms and values of his volume that will make the Constitution come alive for every reader.

Finally, *A More Perfect Union* actually does help make the Constitution come alive because of who the author is. As I learned when I first met him, he has an amazing breadth of expertise beyond medicine. Readers of his earlier books already know of his belief in the importance of education for every American, and we also know of the effectiveness of his Carson Scholars Fund. Now, Americans will also learn that, along with his accomplishments in medicine and education, he has a firm grasp of the rule of law underpinning our country—a pretty remarkable combination for a once underprivileged child from Detroit.

THE CONSTITUTION
AND TODAY'S ISSUES

A QUICK REFERENCE GUIDE

CHAPTER 1
OUR GUIDE TO FREEDOM

"Don't cheat your neighbor by moving the ancient
boundary markers set up by previous generations."
Proverbs 22:28

I have been privileged to travel to more than fifty countries, and each time I return I am more thankful that I was born in the United States. Many ungrateful people like to denigrate our nation. They act as if America were the source of evil in the world and a nation to be escaped, but the large number of people risking life and limb to enter this nation illegally tells a different story. In this nation, people know they can realize their dreams through their own efforts. We can move to any part of the country without permission from someone else. We have freedom to say whatever we want to say and to believe whatever we want to believe.

These liberties we enjoy do not exist by accident. They have not been preserved by luck. We have a governing document, the Constitution of the United States, which outlines the freedoms of the American people and establishes a nation where those freedoms are protected and honored. Written carefully by wise men, our Constitution has stood the test of time, propelling America from a position of obscurity to the highest pinnacle of the world in record time.

As governments of other nations have risen to power, become tyrannical, and fallen, the Constitution and its defenders have kept America on a steady course, free from a government that imposes the will of elites on the people. Countries like France, which has had many revolutions since its initial escape from monarchy in the eighteenth century, have struggled to find stable freedom, but the Constitution has lasted. Guarded carefully by watchful citizens, it stands firm against tyranny of any sort, but it is flexible enough to allow for compromise when necessary. Governed by this document's seven articles, Bill of Rights, and later amendments, America has been safe, stable, and prosperous for more than two hundred years and is going strong.

Students of history will recognize the achievement that the Constitution is. Not only has it lasted, but it inverts the tyrannical patterns that have guided most nations through history. Instead of working to protect those in power, the Constitution defends the people from government encroachments. Instead of setting up ways to monitor citizens, it provides ways of keeping leaders accountable to citizens. Constitutional government recognizes and bows to the will of a godly, educated population. Under the Constitution, our government follows the model set out by Thomas Jefferson: "A wise and frugal government, which shall restrain men from injuring one another, shall leave them otherwise free to regulate their own pursuits of industry and improvement, and shall not take from the mouth of labor the bread it has earned. This is the sum of good government."[1] American government has lasted, and our nation has prospered, specifically because the Constitution has kept the government out of the way.

As James Madison said, "If it be asked what is to restrain the House of Representatives from making legal discriminations in favor of themselves and a particular class of the society? I answer, the genius of the whole system, the nature of just and constitutional laws, and above all the vigilant and manly spirit which actuates the people of America—a spirit which nourishes freedom, and in return is nourished by it."[2] He and the other founders knew that people naturally tend to attempt to enhance their own position and power at the expense of others. This is not a characteristic of one specific race or group of people but is a common weakness among mankind in general.

Recognizing the danger of human nature, our founders wisely created a Constitution that would curtail federal power, building in checks and balances. But they also knew that a good system was not enough. If the people were not vigilant and knowledgeable about the laws and their observation, the government would expand, gradually insinuating itself into every aspect of daily living and eroding Americans' freedoms. Not many years after the Constitution was ratified, Andrew Jackson warned the nation: "But you must remember, my fellow citizens, that eternal vigilance by the people is the price of liberty, and that you must pay the price if you wish to secure the blessing. It behooves you, therefore, to be watchful in your States as well as in the Federal Government."[3]

Sometimes tyranny begins subtly so that only alert citizens can spot it. Many of the founders feared that like so many other societies before us, we would not be vigilant and would allow our freedoms to be taken away by seemingly beneficial laws. Thomas Jefferson warned, "Experience hath shewn, that even under the best forms of government those entrusted with power have, in time, and by slow operations, perverted it into tyranny."[4] For instance, the government may say everyone deserves a college education and announce a program of wealth redistribution in order to make sure that everyone has a fair chance in an increasingly sophisticated world. On the surface this seems like a noble goal and could gain a lot of popular support. The problem with this kind of thinking is that it introduces a type of top-down government that allows a group of elites to determine what is good for the society. It would be wiser to let the society determine what's good for itself and what kind of government it wishes to have through ballot initiatives and through their representatives.

Our founders put a great deal of time, effort, and money into the development of the Constitution. They desperately wanted to ensure that this was not wasted effort and that our government would remain centered on the people. They fully understood that they themselves were highly educated and exceptionally intelligent individuals who had accomplished a great deal in their own right, but they worked to make the Constitution simple enough for everyone. Unlike many of the lengthy and complex bills that are passed by Congress today, our Constitution, not counting the twenty-seven amendments, is less than seventeen pages long. Not only is it small enough to fit in a pocket and short enough to be read in one sitting, but the Constitution is also relatively simple and easy to understand. From the beginning, it was designed to be read by the common people—because the founders knew that the Constitution was for everyone, not just the elite.

The founders were right to take precautions. There is a movement among some elite thinkers today to say that the Constitution is too complicated for the average reader. Some legal scholars insist that the phrases in the Constitution do not mean what they say, and politicians torture the Constitution's vocabulary, distorting its meaning in order to further their own agendas. When an average citizen protests, these elite thinkers respond condescendingly, saying that constitutional scholarship is a matter for experts, not for voters.

Nothing could be further from the truth. While the Constitution is indeed complex, it is simple enough to be understood by anyone with a basic education. While many of the founders were lawyers, many of the signers were businessmen or doctors. If they understood freedom enough to write the Constitution, you shouldn't have to be a lawyer to understand it today.

Unfortunately, the elites may be right in saying that among the average adult population in America, knowledge about how our government actually works is sorely lacking. Compared with the amount of knowledge about civics that was required to obtain a middle-school certificate in the late 1800s (during which time public education ended with a middle-school certificate), the knowledge of most adults today is severely deficient.

This ignorance was one of the founders' worst fears. They were uncertain about the resolve of the American people to maintain a high level of education and interest in the affairs of government. They knew that it would be impossible to preserve the level of liberty being granted to the American people unless the people themselves were a reservoir of knowledge. John Adams said, "Liberty cannot be preserved without a general knowledge among the people."[5] Thomas

Jefferson said, "If a nation expects to be ignorant and free . . . it expects what never was and never will be."[6]

True to Jefferson's prediction, the biggest threat to the maintenance of freedom in America in our time is lack of knowledge. Though almost every American citizen knows that we have a Constitution, few have studied it carefully, and even fewer are standing up to protect it now that it is under attack. Many Americans have never read our governing document, and many are ignorant of the liberties it guarantees and the procedures it has set up. The good news is that this can be remedied. Education is open to all, and the fact that you are reading this book is a good sign that you are ready to become a more informed American citizen. Perhaps you already know and love the Constitution and just want to learn more about it. Or perhaps this is your first effort to educate yourself. Either way, you will find much to inspire you in the following chapters. You will learn about the history of the Constitution and about its framers. You will learn about the Constitution's governing principles as they are laid out in its preamble. You will learn about the structure of the Constitution. Most important, you will learn what you can do to defend it. After all, it is only through the efforts of millions of Americans like you that our "more perfect union" can be preserved for future generations.

CHAPTER 2
HISTORY OF THE CONSTITUTION

"And you will know the truth, and the truth will set you free."

John 8:32

A little knowledge of history can go a long way. I learned this firsthand as a child. When I was thirteen years old, my mother needed to buy a car because our old Oldsmobile was on its last legs. She saved every nickel, dime, and quarter, and to the shock of everyone had the necessary funds to buy a new car when the need arose. This time, though, she considered a used car, which was only one year old and was absolutely beautiful. It was a 1964 convertible Ford Galaxie, black with a red interior. My brother Curtis and I were completely taken with the car, but my mother was somewhat skeptical. With a little research, she was able to discover the history of the vehicle and learned that it was an absolute lemon. If she had bought that car, she would also have bought a lot of heartache.

There is no question that knowing the history of that vehicle improved the quality of our lives. Had we remained ignorant, we might have been duped by the seller. By the same token, it is beneficial for people to know about the history of our Constitution. The Constitution has faced many challenges over the years, and even today there are those who question its validity. No American should accept our Constitution blindly. Instead, we should examine its background and its track record to see where it comes from and whether it holds up. Unlike a used car, the Constitution has proved its reliability repeatedly—and the ideas that oppose it have been proved to be lemons.

Tremendous effort went into the forging of the Constitution, and it is important that we understand why the founders worked so hard to create it. As we learn about their motivations and fears, we will better understand how they meant for us to apply the laws they left us. And the more we learn about the characters and backgrounds of the founders, the better we will understand what kinds of leaders we need to uphold our Constitution and protect the union it created.

THE EARLY COLONIES

The earliest settlers in America wanted to establish governments that provided rights to individuals. Most of them were fleeing monarchies and had strong ideas about how to achieve a free society with freedom of religion. To this end, all of the colonies that populated the eastern seaboard created charters and compacts, and eventually thirteen colonies were established, creating the basis of the future United States of America. Each of these colonies became a state with its own governing body, but they quickly realized that there was a natural interdependence that would enhance their overall strength—a strength they would need if they were to throw off oppression.

Colonial life was difficult and was characterized by disease, injury, and financial hardship. Many people died early deaths, and those who lived worked tirelessly for the sake of their children. When the British Crown began to demand a larger share of the profits earned by American labor, the colonists began to grow resentful. Various skirmishes eventually erupted into a full-fledged revolution as the Americans attempted to break the bonds of servitude. The prospects of victory for the amateur revolutionary forces under the leadership of General George Washington were bleak, considering that they were opposed by the most powerful and professional military force on the planet. Nevertheless, their faith, fortitude, and willingness to perish for their beliefs propelled them to an unlikely victory.

The willingness of the colonies to work together contributed to their surprising success. Although the early associations among the colonies had sometimes been fractious, the colonies did attempt to unite as an official entity, drafting the Articles of Confederation in 1777. The Articles proposed a perpetual union among Massachusetts, New Hampshire, Rhode Island, Connecticut, New York, New Jersey, Pennsylvania, Delaware, Maryland, Virginia, North Carolina, South Carolina, and Georgia. They instituted a Congress composed of representatives from each state, but because each state wanted to maintain its autonomy, the Articles did not give Congress much power over the new nation. Whether it would have any power at all was a real question—the Articles weren't ratified until 1781, though even before ratification they did provide some framework for the assembling states.

Once ratified, the Articles created a central government that could negotiate treaties and organize national defense.

The new government was also supposed to help settle disputes between individual states. Unfortunately, though, the union formed by the Articles was not strong enough.

The new states were fiercely independent, rightly valuing their differences. The needs of each state were different, and the benefit of having a variety of state governments was great. It was this advantage, along with many others, that made the states want to maintain independence from one another. However, early Americans quickly realized that their unity under the Articles was inadequate. They would need a more perfect union.

Because the Articles were written in reaction to Great Britain's overbearing rule, the document focused more on freedom than on finding a way to preserve unity. The Congress that was established by the Articles had legal authority but no way of raising money to fund its actions. Congress's unsecured bills of credit issued for war expenses spiraled to such a low value that they inspired the popular colloquialism "not worth a Continental."[1] Each state had its own currency (Rhode Island printed a huge sum of money that "by law had to be accepted on the same terms as gold"),[2] and some states still wanted to formulate their own foreign policies and international agreements. Congress, meanwhile, could not maintain the peace domestically or internationally, again due to lack of funding.

Accordingly, the states' representatives met to decide what to do, and the Continental Congress resolved on February 21, 1787:

> It is expedient that on the second Monday in May next a Convention of delegates who shall have been appointed by the several States be held at Philadelphia

for the sole and express purpose of revising the Articles of Confederation.[3]

To this end, the states summoned their finest thinkers and leaders, praying that the next convention would provide a solution.

Although the convention was scheduled for the second Monday in May, a quorum of delegates wasn't present until May 25, due to traveling delays caused by heavy spring rains. The group was sequestered in a room for the months of deliberation, and neither the public nor the host city's considerable press corps—nearly a dozen newspapers in all—were permitted to witness the proceedings. The process was labored, and it seemed impossible to obtain agreement on anything.

Twelve of the thirteen states appointed delegates to attend the Constitutional Convention (Rhode Island refused to participate). Of the seventy-four delegates, nineteen declined their appointments. Also missing in action were two notables: Thomas Jefferson, who at the time of the convention was in Paris serving as minister to France; and John Adams, who was minister to Great Britain. That left fifty-five delegates in attendance at the Constitutional Convention, although only thirty-nine of them signed the Constitution.

The delegates represented a generational cross-section of post–Revolutionary War America, with an average age of forty-two. Jonathan Dayton was the youngest at twenty-six while the senior statesman was Benjamin Franklin, who had turned eighty-one that January.[4] Most of the delegates were educated; more than half were college graduates. Their experience in politics was notable: Eight had signed the Declaration of Independence, forty-one had served in the Continental

Congress, and fifteen had worked on drafting state constitutions. Their diversity of backgrounds and occupations is notable, as is their unity on certain themes.

MEN OF OPEN MINDS

While all of the men were patriots, they held a variety of conflicting opinions, and some had even been on the wrong side of the revolution at one point. This shows that they were not ideologues—people who cannot see reason. Instead, these men[5] changed their hearts and minds when they came to understand the benefits of American liberty.

William Samuel Johnson, a fifty-nine-year-old lawyer from Connecticut, had an especially interesting story. A colonial diplomat to Great Britain prior to the war, he generally supported America's ventures toward independence. Yet because his foreign network was so vast, he diligently sought peaceful solutions between the two countries whenever national tempers flared.

Gouverneur Morris grew up surrounded by Loyalists but eventually joined the Whigs and was elected to the revolutionary Provincial Congress of New York (1775–77). He worked with future first chief justice John Jay and fellow lawyer Robert Livingston to draft the original constitution of New York State. He was also one of the shining stars of the youngest generation in the Continental Congress. Well before his thirtieth birthday, he had already signed the historic Articles of Confederation and influenced the framing of the Treaty of Paris, which ended the Revolutionary War. At the Constitutional Convention, Morris made a name for himself with his persuasive and frequent speeches, assuming the podium a record 173 times. He is believed to have written both the preamble and the final draft of the Constitution.

Other delegates, such as George Read of Delaware and John Dickinson of Pennsylvania, had opposed the Declaration of Independence. Dickinson earned the nickname "Penman of the Revolution" for publishing political pieces that spurred his fellow citizens to action against oppressive British policies, yet as a steadfast advocate of peace, his convictions prevented him from signing his country's founding document. Still, recognizing the needs of their nation, these men overcame their doubts in order to help preserve America's freedom. This ability to put aside personal preferences and compromise is seldom seen today.

RICH MEN, POOR MEN

The framers came from different socioeconomic backgrounds. Alexander Hamilton of New York was the illegitimate son of a single mother and grew up relying on charity. Pierce Butler, on the other hand, was born to a baron who was also a member of the British parliament. Despite their differences in wealth, the framers were careful to avoid anything resembling class warfare, keeping any idea of wealth redistribution out of the Constitution.

Many of the framers were familiar with the deleterious effects of class warfare, which was prominent throughout Europe. They hoped that a more egalitarian atmosphere would characterize American culture. They envisioned a country where people would rise and fall based on their abilities and contribution rather than their pedigree. To that end, they put aside their socioeconomic differences and worked together.

MEN OF GOD

Though their beliefs varied, the framers were mostly united in their religious devotion. Delaware delegate Richard Bassett not only was active in the Methodist church but also eagerly played host to numerous religious meetings at his estate in Maryland. Abraham Baldwin of Georgia had been a chaplain in the Continental Army. Many of the framers subscribed to a political theory that viewed all human rights as being derived from God. Therefore, even though the Constitution never mentions God, it was steeped in a Christian understanding of politics.

EDUCATED MEN

Education was also important to the signers, and a glimpse of the lives of a few reveals why. Abraham Baldwin was one of a dozen children born to a blacksmith who had willingly assumed enormous debt in order to put his children through school. When the senior Baldwin died in 1787, Abraham not only paid off the family debts still owed but also, at his own expense, ensured that his siblings could continue their schooling.

George Mason of Virginia was raised by his uncle, who owned one of the largest personal libraries in the colonies. Mason's extensive reading apparently helped to hone his writing skills—among his most notable works were an American defense of the Stamp Act and Virginia's Declaration of

Rights, a document that greatly influenced the Declaration of Independence and the Bill of Rights.

Roger Sherman was a self-educated lawyer and Connecticut businessman who was heavily involved in the convention sessions, and Georgia's William Few was also self-educated. Because they had worked so hard for their educations, these founders valued knowledge and probably expected that future generations of Americans would too.

BUSINESSMEN

The delegates were also diverse in occupation. Though most of them were lawyers, not all were. Jacob Broom, a thirty-five-year-old merchant from Delaware, had studied surveying but had no legal experience to speak of. William L. Pierce of Georgia was a struggling business owner whose primary contribution to history was his notes detailing the business of the convention sessions and his "character sketches" of the men who attended.

Many capitalism-minded delegates used their businesses to serve their country. John Langdon owned a mercantile, but during the war he built armed ships for American use. Due to lack of state-approved funding, Langdon paid for himself and delegate Nicholas Gilman to attend the Constitutional Convention on behalf of New Hampshire. Though they came late to the proceedings, Langdon's speeches and committee involvement proved invaluable.

An orphaned George Clymer of Pennsylvania was taken in and educated by a rich uncle in the mercantile trade. The lad was an eager learner who worked his way up to partner, inherited the business upon his uncle's death, and later negotiated a successful merger with the Meredith firm. Clymer's patriotic activism was influenced by the impact of British sanctions on trade with American businesses. He ultimately assumed the role of continental treasurer and in effect financed the war effort with his own funds. After representing Pennsylvania at the Second Continental Congress (1780–82), Clymer was a state legislator from 1784 to 1788.

Robert Morris, born near Liverpool, England, never set foot on American soil until he was a teenager. Though his father exported tobacco from their home in Maryland, Robert joined a prosperous shipping/banking company owned by father and son Thomas and Charles Willing. At age twenty Morris was named a partner in the firm, and he remained with the company into his sixties. During his three years with the First Continental Congress and beyond, he proved to be the right man at the right time in the political realm.

From 1781 to 1784 Morris undertook the position of superintendent of finance. To get the new government on sound economic footing, Morris imposed drastic spending cuts on all fronts and demanded financial accountability at the federal and state levels. He sacrificed personally when the nation needed it too, funding military purchases out of his own pocket and assuming government debt in his own name. Perhaps most notably, Morris secured a pivotal loan from the French in his first year as superintendent. This money simultaneously funded both General Washington's forces at the Battle of Yorktown (a turning point that finally persuaded Great Britain to begin serious negotiations with America for its independence) and America's first federally incorporated bank (assisted by some of Morris's own investment). His business acumen, along with that of his convention colleagues, was critical to the fledgling country's economic success.

SOLDIERS

Many of the delegates had served in the Revolutionary War, including Thomas Mifflin. Mifflin was born into a Quaker family in Philadelphia and graduated from the city's college (now the University of Pennsylvania) in 1760 at age sixteen. He succeeded in several business ventures, but his heart was with the colonial cause. In spite of his religious upbringing, Mifflin not only mustered troops but also led them beginning in 1775—and was promptly expelled from his church. His service as a personal assistant, or aide-de-camp, to George Washington springboarded him to appointment as the first quartermaster general of the Continental Army, an executive position behind the lines overseeing the commanders in the field and the supply of the war effort, among other duties. Being a man of action, he wasn't particularly fulfilled in this role. He did engage in battles in New York and New Jersey, however, and before he resigned he earned the rank of major general. He also served for a time as president of the Second Continental Congress.

DOCTORS

Not only were there businessmen and soldiers among the delegates, but there were also several doctors. Five doctors had signed the Declaration of Independence, and as highly educated individuals they were deeply involved in local and national affairs during the early days of our nation.

There are many today who think that doctors should stick to medicine and cannot possibly know anything about any other area of life. The opposite is true: Most doctors are deeply invested in areas of knowledge besides medicine. In fact, today's medical schools actively seek out students who are not confined to traditional premed majors like the biological sciences. History and philosophy majors as well as a variety of others are welcomed with open arms and are taught, like everyone else, to make decisions based on evidence rather than on ideology.

When we undertake policy making in this nation, we can benefit only when we are willing to hear the voices of a variety of citizens from different professions, including medicine. When doctors began to retreat from the public square to their operating rooms, laboratories, and clinics, leaving the social welfare of their patients in the hands of bureaucrats, health care began to transform from a social obligation to a business. Clearly patients will be the beneficiaries when those making the important policy decisions are also those who are concerned and knowledgeable about their health and well-being.

James McHenry of Maryland was one of the physicians at the convention. The Irish-born McHenry was educated in Dublin but set off for America on his own at age eighteen and was joined by his family the following year. While the family started a Baltimore-based business, McHenry studied under physician Benjamin Rush and then signed on as a military surgeon until he was captured as a prisoner of war at Fort Washington. As soon as he could return to service (1778), he joined George Washington at Valley Forge and subsequently served the Marquis de Lafayette until elected to the Maryland Senate, where he represented his constituents from 1781 to 1786 and again from 1791 to 1796.

Hugh Williamson of North Carolina studied for the ministry and worked as a college professor before choosing his long-term line of work. A member of the first graduating class of the College of Philadelphia (now the University of Pennsylvania) in 1757, he would cross the ocean a few years later, having decided to pursue a medical degree. After returning to Philadelphia to set up practice, Williamson soon wearied of medicine but became known for his studies in astronomy, which included penning "An Essay on Comets" in 1771 and tracking the movements of Mercury and Venus.

An eyewitness to the Boston Tea Party, he testified before a British council that revolt was brewing in America. When his warnings proved true, and the first shots of the revolution were fired, Williamson came home and reestablished his medical practice. North Carolina's governor ultimately enlisted him as surgeon general to the militia. He is especially remembered for his pioneering efforts to mitigate illness within the fighting ranks by applying a number of hygienic methods. After the war, Williamson also served in his state legislature, the U.S. House of Representatives, and the Continental Congress.

Native-born Virginian James McClurg was an internationally renowned physician whose medical writings brought him much attention within the scientific community. He earned his medical degree from the University of Edinburgh (Scotland) and did postgraduate work in Paris and London. In addition to his wartime surgical work, he served as president of the Virginia Medical Society in his later years and as a medical professor for a time at his alma mater, the College of William and Mary. Like that of the other physicians among the signers, his expertise helped ground the Constitutional Convention.

LEADERS

As the convention progressed, some delegates began to stand out as leaders. Twenty-nine-year-old lawyer and planter Charles Pinckney from South Carolina considered himself the greatest among his peers, speaking frequently during the Constitutional Convention and often problem solving as he spoke. His claim that he drafted the source document for the U.S. Constitution has been refuted. Nevertheless, his work on the final draft was substantial, and he used his influence to ratify the Constitution in his home state in 1788. He would later become a three-time governor of South Carolina and be elected to the U.S. Senate and House of Representatives.

James Madison was another prominent delegate. The Virginian had studied government, law, and theology at the College of New Jersey (now Princeton). Afterward he returned home and involved himself in local politics, being named a delegate to the Virginia Convention (1776). There he helped to create the state constitution. He also served twice in the Virginia House.

Even though he was one of the youngest members of the First Continental Congress, he was recognized as a change agent. His impact extended to the Constitutional Convention, where his copious writings on the limiting qualities of the Articles of Confederation, along with his more than 150 addresses to the 1787 assembly, hastened the work.

Madison was the brains behind the Virginia Plan, a key basis for our current Constitution, and his convention journal affords us an unsurpassed record of these historic sessions. He also was a point man in seeing the Constitution through the Continental Congress.

By the time he arrived to preside over the convention, George Washington was already well known for his victorious command of the Continental Army. Recognizing the ineffectiveness of the Articles of Confederation, Washington, along with Madison and others, favored a unifying central government, and he promoted this ideal in his dignified way during the proceedings.

Perhaps the most famous delegate was Benjamin Franklin, whose limited formal education did not stop him from becoming one of history's most highly regarded thinkers and inventors and a heralded diplomat on two continents. After apprenticing with his father, who made soap and candles, as a boy he began working with his older half-brother James in the printing business. James had founded one of the first newspapers in the colonies, the *New-England Courant*, and without any fanfare the periodical included young Benjamin's first published essays.

Due to disagreements with his brother, Benjamin relocated to Philadelphia in 1723, continuing as a printer with another company for a year before moving to London. Not long after his return to Philadelphia, he took over the *Pennsylvania Gazette* (1730–48). However, his annual publication *Poor Richard's Almanack* (1732–58) was what put him on the literary map. It was such an overwhelming success that only the Bible was read by more colonists. With this early-American best seller came financial independence. While Franklin nurtured his interests in science and politics, his philanthropic efforts established hospitals, libraries, and schools.

Franklin's first foray into politics was in 1736, when he was appointed a clerk of the colonial legislature. He was subsequently elected as a member, serving from 1751 to 1764.

Among his various positions in local government was deputy postmaster of Philadelphia (1737–53). He fulfilled a similar role for all the colonies from 1753 to 1774.

It was during an eleven-year stint in England as a representative of various colonies that Franklin's eyes were opened to the revolutionary cause, especially when he recognized the tyranny of the Stamp Act. He worked tirelessly for its repeal, and through these efforts became one of America's leading defenders of freedom. (He also did considerable work in his twilight years to abolish slavery.)

Franklin returned home once more and set to work at the Continental Congress, and in June of 1776 he helped to draft the Declaration of Independence. However, diplomatic duties drew him back to Europe later that year, and he directed various political negotiations with France as a commissioner between 1776 and 1785. His landmark achievement in that role was his collaboration with John Adams and John Jay to facilitate the war-ending Treaty of Paris in 1783.

Back on American soil, though hindered by ill health and age, he attended most sessions of the Constitutional Convention and frequently intervened to quell disputes—a leader among leaders to the final day.

CONFLICT

Although the delegates were largely cooperative and cordial, there was plenty of conflict. Luther Martin of Maryland, a vocal opponent of a centralized government, stood before the assembly arguing against the Virginia Plan for more than three hours. The debate was so heated that Martin and fellow

Maryland delegate John Mercer left the convention. Martin actually fought ratification of the Constitution afterward.

The Virginia Plan favored states with large populations and advocated for a bicameral (two-chamber) legislature. The plan called for each state to have proportional representation in each of the legislative bodies. Of course this did not appeal to the states with small populations, since they would be dramatically overpowered by larger states like Virginia. The New Jersey Plan, in contrast, advocated for a unicameral (one-chamber) legislature in which each state would have a single vote regardless of its size and population. The dispute over the two plans was so significant that it threatened to derail the whole process of creating a union. Fortunately, the so-called Great Compromise resolved this conflict by suggesting a bicameral legislature with a House of Representatives that was populated on a proportional basis and a Senate that gave equal votes to each state.

Alexander Hamilton of New York was a major figure in the conflict, pushing a self-named plan that he deemed able to accomplish what neither the Virginia Plan nor the New Jersey Plan could. Delegate William Pierce said of Hamilton, "There is no skimming over the surface of a subject with him, he must sink to the bottom to see what foundation it rests on."[6] Despite his thoroughness, though, Hamilton's plan was rejected.

The fight over the New Jersey Plan and the Virginia Plan wasn't the only disagreement. There were intense arguments between the Federalists and the Anti-Federalists before the Constitution was finally ratified by the requisite number of states in 1788. The Federalists wanted a powerful central government. Their primary advocates were Alexander Hamilton,

James Madison, and John Jay, who became the first chief justice of the Supreme Court. They went so far as to write a series of pro-Constitution essays known as *The Federalist Papers*, in which they eloquently laid out the argument for a strong federal government and indicated how it would work. Many of the papers were published in newspapers throughout the country and played an important role in the ratification of our Constitution.

The Anti-Federalists were just as vocal in their opposition to a strong central government and also wrote a series of papers that were widely disseminated. Their principal concern was that a strong central government would become more like a monarchy and would usurp the power of the people over time. They particularly wanted to prevent the executive branch from becoming too powerful. They eventually assented to the creation of a strong central government, but they insisted on countering it with the first ten amendments to the Constitution, otherwise known as the Bill of Rights. These amendments gave the people strong and specific protections that were not clearly spelled out in the original articles.

In retrospect, both groups were right. The Federalists were correct in predicting that a strong central government would promote the development of a strong nation. Federalism's economic synergies throughout the nation would create a strong middle class and a powerful economic engine.

On the other hand, the Anti-Federalists correctly predicted that the strong federal government would usurp the power of the states and make them subservient. Fortunately, the Bill of Rights, for which they were responsible, has shielded us from further encroachments on freedom.

Once the Constitution was ratified by the states (a two-thirds majority was the requirement), George Washington was the unanimous electoral-college choice for president in 1789. Intent on providing the inexperienced nation with some much-needed grounding, he traveled throughout the Northeast that year and the South in 1791, in an effort to inform and unify his countrymen regarding the development of and need for the Constitution. The people who lived closer to the capital had been privy to the evolution of this essential document all along. Not so those who lived in more distant regions. And Washington wanted to even the playing field. Today our leaders would do well to learn from Washington's example of protecting both unity and diversity.

LOOKING FOR TODAY'S LEADERS

Our Constitution was founded by brave and wise men, leaders who had America's best interests at heart. They knew firsthand the pains of living under tyranny, and they sacrificed much in order to ensure that we, their descendants, would not suffer the same way. Their hard work has paid off, as the Constitution has so far stood the test of time. We should seek to honor their legacy by upholding its principles and emulating their unselfish examples.

The Constitution's history also teaches us much about the types of leaders we should seek out. The founders had diverse backgrounds, but they tended to be people of accomplishment with real-world experience. Many of them demonstrated that a life filled with political experience was not a prerequisite for brilliant thinking and effective leadership. Instead of continuing to view political experience as the main criterion for a leader, we should instead examine political candidates to see if they understand America's history. We should draw leaders from all walks of life—business, the military, the church, and medicine. We should look for leaders who have open minds and are able to deal well with conflict. We should follow statesmen who value education. Most of all, we should make sure that we elect only leaders who understand the principles of the Constitution, which we will examine in the next section of this book.

THE SACRED PRINCIPLES

"We the People of the United States, in Order to form a more perfect Union, establish Justice, insure domestic Tranquility, provide for the common defence, promote the general Welfare, and secure the Blessings of Liberty to ourselves and our Posterity, do ordain and establish this Constitution for the United States of America."

This preamble is the Constitution's introductory statement and sets forth the general principles and goals of our governmental structure. It reveals the hearts of the founders and lays out their goals. It's the "why" behind the "what" and "how" of the rest of the Constitution, and without it we would have difficulty understanding why the delegates wrote the Constitution as they did.

Although the entire Constitution, including amendments, is less than twenty pages long, many have written thousands of pages analyzing and explaining it. Some of this commentary is useful, but much of it needlessly complicates what is straightforward. If you accept the Constitution's words at face value, it is relatively easy to understand. If you want to reinterpret its words in order to make its meaning fit your ideology, you will have to do a lot of explaining. Fortunately, the preamble helps prevent this kind of misinterpretation and overcomplication by telling us the Constitution's overarching goals. If we understand the purpose of the Constitution, it will be harder to be fooled by ideologues who want to twist its words. Instead of following their arguments through all of their twists and turns, we can identify the goal of their interpretation, compare it with the Constitution's goals, and decide whether the two match.

Before you begin any study of the Constitution's provisions, it is important to meditate on its main goals. What does it mean to be part of "We the People"? What does "a more perfect Union" look like? Who decides what constitutes the "general Welfare"? Most important, how do we preserve the liberty we've inherited so that future generations can enjoy it? Only by embracing the founders' concepts of justice and tranquillity will we be able to uphold the Constitution in the right way and for the right reasons.

Every American should memorize the preamble and keep its principles in mind while voting. If we elect only officials who understand the Constitution and its goals, America's future will be safe.

CHAPTER 3
WE THE PEOPLE

"Take a lesson from the ants, you lazybones. Learn from their ways and become wise! Though they have no prince or governor or ruler to make them work, they labor hard all summer, gathering food for the winter."

Proverbs 6:6–8

"We the People of the United States" are the first words of the Constitution. These words distinguished our government from the many other governments of the world. Many of those nations allowed—and still allow—small groups of elites or a royal family to control the lives of the common people. Our founders had experienced that kind of tyranny, and their first order of business in the Constitution was to prevent it from creeping into the new government. They decreed that the American government always be controlled by the will of the people, not the people by the will of the government. All of the articles and amendments of the Constitution that follow the preamble are dedicated to keeping "we the People" in charge.

"We the People" includes all citizens, both those by birth and those legalized through the immigration processes. Today, unlike in the early days of America, everyone may attain citizenship, regardless of their financial status, ethnicity, gender, or heritage. No one is considered superior or inferior to the rest of the population. Every American is part of the body of voters that rules the country, and no vote is unimportant.

This egalitarian approach is one of the hallmarks of fairness in America and must always be maintained. Unfortunately, "we the People" are often quick to give up our liberties. We quickly forget that many people were willing to give their lives and their resources so that future Americans could be free and empowered. Because so much was sacrificed by so many to provide a nation in which we the people are in charge, we must continue to actively combat all attempts to empower the government at the expense of the people. We exercise our power and fight government encroachment by knowing our rights, being vigilant, voting, and speaking up.

EXERCISING POWER BY KNOWING YOUR RIGHTS

Knowing the law can make all the difference in how you are treated, individually or as a society. I saw the truth of this one time when I was a student at Yale and returned home to Michigan during a break. While there, my family attended a special camp meeting in a rural area, and we parked in a nearby grass lot. Upon returning to the car, we noticed that everyone's license plates had been removed, supposedly by the landowner, who had left a note informing us where we could retrieve them. At the pickup location I found a long line of people paying stiff fines in order to retrieve their license plates. Since there were no signs prohibiting parking in the lot, I investigated and learned that the people removing the license plates were not the landowners and were not government officials. I informed the collectors that by law they were unauthorized to remove state-issued plates and that I would call the state troopers unless they not only returned the plates immediately but also replaced them on the cars. They quickly complied, because I knew the law and so did they. They had been illegally tampering with the license plates in order to make a profit off people who were ill informed.

Similarly, if the American people and their representatives do not know and understand what is in our Constitution, others will take advantage of them. Only when we understand the law of our land can we effectively hold our representatives accountable. Knowledge is power, and we must refuse to be bullied.

EXERCISING POWER BY BEING VIGILANT

Once we understand the Constitution and our rights, we must be vigilant to make sure our leaders uphold those rights. People who are otherwise reasonable and fair can sometimes be corrupted by power, and the longer they have that power, the more corrupt they become. John Adams put it this way: "There is danger from all men. The only Maxim of a free government ought to be to trust no man living with power to endanger the public liberty."[1] We must carefully monitor the actions of anyone we empower through the ballot box, because the power might corrupt them. Sometimes a mere gentle reminder of what abuse of power looks like will be enough to rein in an official. In other cases it might be necessary to recall a representative or vote them out of office in the next election cycle.

It is important to remember that it is a natural human tendency to accrue power and try to dominate others. When we realize this, we will be less likely to demonize those who engage in such activities. On the other hand, we should in no way condone power grabs or manipulation of our Constitution by anyone, regardless of their political affiliation. This is where American values trump partisan politics, and this must always be the case if we are to maintain rule by the people. As soon as we begin overlooking abuse of power by an official who is a member of our own party, we become part of the problem.

Because of our current representatives' corruption, many Americans no longer trust the federal government. Some refuse to analyze the reasons for this distrust and prefer to think about other things, like sports, entertainment, and lifestyles of the rich and famous. We have the choice of continuing to be distracted by trivialities or of faithfully watching for and responding to abuse of the Constitution. If we choose the former option, our descendants will be faced with much less pleasant options.

When we the people do our job, we pay attention to how our representatives vote. We compare what they say with what they do. We hold people of both parties accountable. We refuse to succumb to apathy or trust others to monitor for us. And we turn that vigilance into action.

EXERCISING POWER BY VOTING

American citizens need to remember that members of Congress serve at our pleasure and can be voted out of office anytime the electorate becomes dissatisfied with their performance. The founders anticipated that the federal government would have to be reined in by average American citizens who were willing to educate themselves and vote intelligently.

"We the People" of America are actually at the pinnacle of power. We need not feel like victims or that things are out of our hands. America can become a land characterized by despotism only if the people relinquish their power as voters. Apathy has destroyed other nations before ours, and it can destroy this nation as well if we neglect to involve ourselves in elections.

Our power resides in informed voting. Informed voting isn't voting the party line or voting based on what political pundits say or on what friends and family tell you to do, but rather voting based on your own values and principles. It means actually taking the time to think about what you believe and what is important to you. It means knowing who your congressional representatives are and how they have voted. Not how they claim they have voted, but how they have actually voted. (There are excellent resources available to obtain this information, including free online resources in my book *One Vote*.)

We must remember that freedom is not free. We have to regard it as a prized possession that must be fought for and protected every day. If preserving freedom means spending time researching politicians, so be it. If it means remembering to vote in local elections, do what it takes to remind yourself. If it means going to the nursing home and getting your bedridden grandmother registered to vote by absentee ballot, so be it. If you need to help her fill it out, help her fill it out. If we are lazy, fearful, or uncaring, all that so many have fought for will be lost, and our children and grandchildren will suffer the consequences.

EXERCISING POWER BY SPEAKING UP

Finally, we the people exercise power by speaking our minds. Many of the early patriots in our nation had experienced tyranny that prevented them from expressing their opinions. They could not speak against the king or against the established church. They knew that America's citizens would need to be free to express themselves if they were to rule. Thus they set in place the Constitution's First Amendment, guaranteeing the freedom of speech and expression.

We've preserved this freedom so that our government doesn't usually try to prevent the people from speaking. Recognizing this achievement, many assert that there is no restriction of speech in the United States and that everyone is completely free to express themselves. Unfortunately, this is a naive claim. Today the political correctness (PC) police are the biggest threat to America's freedom of speech, and they are doing their best to squelch the opinions of "we the People."

There is not an officially established PC police force, but its members exist in government, throughout the media, in educational institutions, etc. Members of the PC police are those who carefully monitor the speech and behavior of anyone they consider to be a threat to their leftist ideological domination. The PC police do not care that people disagree with them, as long as those people remain silent. But if someone openly disagrees with them, they demonize that person with ridicule and infantile name-calling. This kind of speech policing has created fear in a large portion of our populace, causing them to remain silent rather than face the repercussions of expressing themselves honestly.

When people become reluctant to express themselves because they may be persecuted or ostracized, they almost might as well be living under a tyrannical government. This repression can be stopped only if large portions of the American population are committed to speaking out against attempts to shut down freedom of expression. For instance, when we hear about a local school trying to take the words "under God" out of the Pledge of Allegiance, we should personally get involved in voicing our opposition to such censorship.

Recently, teachers in Lincoln, Nebraska, were told not to refer to pupils as "boys" or "girls" because it is bad to teach students gender disparity.[2] I believe this is taking political correctness to another level of absurdity, and I have loudly voiced my opposition to such foolishness. The vast majority of Americans understand that there is a difference between male and female—and long live the difference, which adds to the spice of life. It is eminently possible to recognize that there is a difference between boys and girls without introducing sexism or any other type of unfairness. It is much better to deal with these issues logically and with respect for tradition than through the emotional lens of the politically correct ideology of the moment. Introducing a speech code or stifling traditionalists—or failing to speak up when others do—is not the way to go.

Whatever the dangers, remaining silent is a huge mistake on the part of those desirous of freedom. Ayn Rand put it this way: "Do not keep silent when your own ideas and values are being attacked. . . . If a dictatorship ever comes to this country, it will be by the default of those who keep silent. We are still free enough to speak. Do we have time? No one can tell."[3] If we allow ourselves to be cowed by the PC police, we are the ones to blame for the bad policies that result.

It is not just the fear of speaking one's opinion that is eroding freedom in our nation, but also the fear of retaliation for contributing to organizations that are targeted by government agencies like the Internal Revenue Service. In 2013 the IRS finally admitted that it screened organizations' tax-exemption applications for terms like "tea party" and "patriotic," targeting groups using those words for closer scrutiny. The IRS claimed that this type of targeting was evenhanded and only coincidentally appeared to be aimed at conservative groups. The media tried to make the scandal into a political issue between Democrats and Republicans, but it should be offensive to anyone in favor of freedom in America. Even though politicians and portions of the media will attempt to sweep this dark episode in American history under the rug, the American people must be vigilant and make certain that this affront to freedom is never forgotten. Justice dictates that we get to the bottom of this illegal action and make sure that it never occurs again.

Although the First Amendment protects us from the PC

police in government, it does not give us a way to rid ourselves of their influence in other sectors. Fortunately, their only real weapon is intimidation, so we can gain enormous freedom by simply ignoring them and expressing ourselves with the same kind of courage that characterized our ancestors. Courage begets courage, and a few brave citizens can inspire others to stand up and join civil conversations about tough issues. It is these discussions that will result in societal advancement, particularly when both sides can speak without fear of intimidation or reprisals. On the other hand, guarded conversations between people with different opinions severely limit the likelihood of progress being made.

Many will completely agree with all of the preceding statements but will fear there is nothing they can do as individual concerned citizens. This fear is misguided. You can make a difference if you stop being afraid to speak up. Speak with the full knowledge that our Constitution protects your speech. If there are repercussions, seek legal recourse and voice your complaints. If enough people begin to do this, it will have a chilling effect on the PC police and eventually these people will begin to reform their ways. You can also make your congressional representatives aware of the oppression of free speech you have observed. When they see a pattern, they will be encouraged to take up the fight on your behalf. This is the way our representative government was designed, but it only works when there is active participation by the people.

Protecting the rule of the people means having open and frank discussions with people in your sphere of influence about what kind of nation we want to pass on to the next generation and what we are willing to do to preserve it. This is exactly what our ancestors did in the prerevolutionary days of America. By speaking with one another about the tyranny they were experiencing under the British, they gained the courage to act against King George III and his overwhelming forces.

PRESERVING OUR POWER

Our Constitution was established to ensure the permanent freedom of the American people, not to provide guidelines for management of the people by the government. The American people will decide the destiny of America, and that decision is a weighty responsibility. It is sobering when looking through the annals of history to notice how many free societies became subject to brutal tyranny in a short period of time because people were not paying attention or simply refused to believe that their freedom was in jeopardy. As former president and great patriot Ronald Reagan said, "Freedom is a fragile thing and is never more than one generation away from extinction. It is not ours by inheritance; it must be fought for and defended constantly by each generation, for it comes only once to a people."[4]

Historically Americans have not been quitters. We may not always be right, but we have always fought for our beliefs with bravery and strength. It was that kind of bravery that allowed us to prevail over the Axis powers during World War II and to achieve an even less likely victory over the British in the Revolutionary War.

There will be ups and downs, but we can never despair or give up. We now are the keepers of the flame of liberty and justice for all. As he left the Constitutional Convention, Ben Franklin was asked what kind of government the founders had created. "A republic, if you can keep it,"[5] he responded. By the grace of God, we will not only keep our republic and preserve our freedom but also enhance it for those following us and for all of humanity.

CHAPTER 4
IN ORDER TO FORM
A MORE PERFECT UNION

"A house is built by wisdom and becomes strong through
good sense. Through knowledge its rooms are filled with
all sorts of precious riches and valuables."

Proverbs 24:3–4

Unity improves almost every situation. I saw this firsthand in the medical field. I was fortunate to train as a neurosurgeon at the Johns Hopkins Medical Institutions, where many of the neurosurgeons were some of the most highly regarded medical practitioners in history. The neurology department at Hopkins was well known, as was the psychiatry department. Each department had highly effective administrators and support staff who contributed to their greatness. In the seventies some of the new leaders in these departments began to recognize that if they combined their administrations, they might achieve significant cost savings and improvements in efficiency. The medical school and the university agreed, and the concept of a neuroscience center was born. The rest is history, as the neuroscience studies at Johns Hopkins achieved worldwide recognition. The strength that was gained through unity was much greater than the individual strength of each separate department.

Recognizing the power of unity, the Constitution's framers wrote in the preamble that they desired to "form a more perfect Union." Our nation had begun as a loosely associated collection of states, each of which acted like a small nation unto itself. There was no central authority to coordinate the collective defense or to facilitate mutually beneficial commercial activities. This left the states vulnerable and directionless in a dangerous world of greedy, predatory nations.

One of the main purposes of the Constitution was to form an effective union that balanced unity and liberty. The founders of our country recognized that there was tremendous synergy and strength to be gained if the states were united in a meaningful way. Not only would they have a better chance of thwarting attacks by other nations, but they would also have significantly more power when negotiating treaties and trade agreements throughout the world. This union had to be strong enough to provide a united front.

The union also had to be weak enough not to deprive the individual states of the right to govern themselves. Large states and small states had different needs. Industrial states wanted different rules from agricultural states. Southerners and Yankees thought each other were inferior. A more perfect union would have to be weak enough to allow the states to make their own decisions on some matters.

But before the delegates could unite the states they would need to overcome their own disunity. Many of them disagreed strongly on the details of how the Constitution should be structured. If they could not stop bickering about these individual points, there would be no hope of forging any Constitution at all.

Fortunately, the delegates had two strategies. First, they made the Constitution as broad as possible, leaving out details that might cause disagreement. By doing this they made room for compromise and calmed themselves enough to work together. Second, they gave the federal government supreme power—but only in a limited number of areas. This would allow the states enough sovereignty to tailor their governing styles to their individual needs. By avoiding being bogged down in details and by balancing strength and liberty, the delegates created a true union—one more perfect than that effected by the Articles of Confederation.

ESCAPING THE DETAILS TRAP

Sometimes people get so bogged down in the details and risks of a situation that they miss the big picture that mandates action. I well remember the case of a little girl from Connecticut who fell off a swing in the schoolyard and hit her head, experiencing a postconcussive seizure as a result. No one was overly concerned until she started developing increasingly frequent seizures, up to sixty per day despite medications. After multiple medical consultations, she ended up at Johns Hopkins, where I and the neurology team concluded that she was a candidate for a major surgical procedure to stop the seizures.

After I explained to her parents the risks of surgery, they decided that they would try to live with the seizures. I understood their fear of the risks, but the decision to avoid these potential problems meant that their daughter would be stuck with guaranteed problems—and still not out of danger. I feared that their concern over the surgical risks had kept them from seeing the big picture.

Then that Christmas she had a grand mal seizure. That was enough to persuade her parents to proceed with the surgery despite the risks. Although the surgery went well, she remained in a coma for four weeks, during which time her parents were beside themselves with grief and guilt. Fortunately, she awakened and made a tremendous recovery and even became a model student at school. This would never have happened if she had not had the surgery and if her parents had continued to focus on the risks instead of the big picture. Similarly, those who penned our Constitution focused on the big concepts rather than getting bogged down in minutiae that would have led to endless battles and inaction.

One of the outstanding features of the Constitution is its lack of details. The preamble declares the document's purpose, and the body of the document provides the structures and mechanisms for governance, all without being overly concerned with every detail of implementation. The framers didn't describe what "the general Welfare" looked like or set out exactly how national defense should work. They wanted to concentrate on broad concepts rather than minutiae, because they realized that the nation would change and that the little details would have to be changed frequently. Constant squabbling over such details would have been detrimental to our national interests.

Even with the lack of details, there are still many in Congress who simply like to argue over everything without getting much of anything done. They do not seem to realize that some of the problems facing our nation currently, such as a huge national debt, stagnant wages, a demoralized military, a failing public school system, poor access to medical care, and an abysmal business environment, to name a few, are so substantial that if we don't address them adequately in the near future, the little details over which they are squabbling will become irrelevant.

As citizens, we need to get beyond squabbling with one another about tactics. For example, instead of arguing about how fast the debt should be reduced, we should unite on the common ground that it ought to be reduced at all. As we fight over details, our children's future is worsening. It's time to focus on common ground and take swift action based on our agreement before our nation moves beyond saving.

BALANCING FEDERAL AND STATE POWERS

Once the framers agreed to work together, they had to figure out how to create a system that united the states without trampling on the rights of state governments. Arizona's recent experience with illegal immigration illustrates the importance of this balance of unity and liberty. In 2010 the governor of the state tried to enforce already existent immigration laws, because the state was being flooded with illegal immigrants from south of the border. The federal government, deciding for reasons of its own that it did not want the border laws enforced, initiated a legal action against the state. It is questionable whether that kind of federal interference helps to establish a more perfect union. Fortunately, our system is designed to prevent the federal government from trampling on the rights of states with impunity. The state could file a countersuit, have its legislative branch produce new legislation, or wait for the judicial branch to strike down unwarranted federal intervention.

The founders feared that the central government, once it had united the states, would become too powerful and would impose its will upon the people—or the individual states—without regard to their wishes. This "government knows best" model was one that they were quite familiar with from their extensive studies of other governmental models as well as from their personal experience with the British monarchy. They felt that their best defense against a tyrannical government was to divide the power three ways, with each branch of government having the power to check the other two. They also listed the powers that the federal government would have, being sure to leave the balance of power in the hands of the states and the people. They wisely concluded that the states would not be eager to give additional power to the federal government and limited its power accordingly.

Unfortunately, the founders did not realize that the time would come when the federal government would approve a federal taxation system that could control the states by giving or withholding financial resources. Such an arrangement significantly upsets the balance of power between the states and the federal government. As a result, today there are numerous social issues, such as the legalization of marijuana, gay marriage, and welfare reform, that could probably be more efficiently handled at the state level but with which the federal government keeps interfering. The states, instead of standing up for their rights, comply with the interference because they want federal funds. It will require noble leaders at the federal level and courageous leaders at the state level to restore the balance of power, but it is essential that such balance be restored for the sake of the people.

DANGERS OF AN IMPERFECT UNION

As the founders feared, the federal government has become much too large and much too powerful. It has usurped responsibilities that belong to the state governments, and as a result it taxes and spends far more than it should. The lion's share of the gross domestic output is consumed by the federal government and its many programs. For a large number of Americans, particularly those who are well-to-do, federal income taxes are their greatest annual expense, in many cases more than double their annual mortgage expense. This is a natural consequence of ever-expanding government. Legislators who feed at the public trough have no desire to curtail that feeding and keep the taxing and spending going. To compound the problem, our government is expanding by borrowing from the futures of our children.

The obvious problem of mounting debt should inspire our government to unity, but so far it has not. Although each branch of the federal government should bear some responsibility for our overwhelming federal debt, our leaders seem only to engage in finger-pointing and passing the buck. They need to understand that they all have different roles to play but that they are on the same team.

Our government can be compared to the game of chess, where on each side there are several kinds of pieces that move in different ways but are all focused on the same ultimate goal. I was on the chess team both in high school and in college, and I learned a lot of strategies that combined the strengths of different pieces to win the game. Failure to understand these strategies frequently led to a stalemate or a draw when in fact there was plenty of firepower to win the game. Similarly, unless both parties and all branches of our federal government recognize that we have departed from the original intent of the Constitution and work together, true union and its attendant freedom and prosperity will be a distant reality.

Under an imperfect union, we have steadily increased the diet of taxpayer money and grown the government to an unmanageable and inefficient size. The federal government constantly attempts to control every aspect of our lives. Many politicians seem to feel entitled to take our resources regardless of how hard we worked for them, believing that they have the right to redistribute them to other citizens.

Thomas Jefferson would not have agreed with such ideas; he wrote, "The true foundation of republican government is the equal right of every citizen in his person and property, and in their management."[1] He and, I'm certain, the rest of the founders would have been horrified to see a federal government trying to regulate the foods that we serve our children or the type of care that we can receive from our doctors, to name just two examples. This is not to say that government shouldn't play some role in public-safety issues and civil matters, but the Constitution makes it clear that in most cases those things should be handled at the state level rather than at the federal level.

There was a specific reason for empowering the states rather than the federal government to deal with civil issues. Namely, a federal judge can, as we have seen recently, overturn the will of the people without facing any repercussions. It is much more difficult for state judges to ignore the will of the people. Since our country was designed around the will of the people, this is an exceedingly important issue that will need to be addressed in the near future if the people are to retain power. Having a ballot referendum on an important issue is a farce if a federal judge can throw out the results and impose his or her own will in place of the will of the people. Unless these kinds of actions truly upset the populace, and unless the people are willing to actively involve themselves in restoring the balance of power, our carefully balanced union will turn into tyranny, and self-determination by the people will become only a distant memory.

PRESERVING THE UNION

Although our Constitution is not perfect, it set up a good balance of power and has worked quite well so far, but it will do us no good if the American people don't uphold it. The more perfect union has lasted, but today it is deteriorating. In one sense our union is too weak, as politicians squabble about details and can't take action even as our nation heads toward disaster. In another sense the union is too strong, because the federal government has taken too much power from the states. Our goal today should be to follow the founders' example. We must compromise for the sake of the big picture, and we must return power to the states. Only by doing that will we return to being a "more perfect Union."

CHAPTER 5
ESTABLISH JUSTICE AND
ENSURE DOMESTIC TRANQUILLITY

"Those who control their tongue will have a long life;
opening your mouth can ruin everything."

Proverbs 13:3

We live in a world in desperate need of justice and domestic tranquillity. In the summer of 2014 in Missouri, an eighteen-year-old black male was shot and killed by a white police officer. A local grand jury composed of mixed races decided not to indict the officer. Crowds disagreeing with the decision rioted. The riots spread throughout the country, causing incredible destruction, while Americans argued over what true justice was.

One group of citizens argued that the teenager seemed likely to have been involved in a recent strong-arm robbery and had attacked the police officer, attempting to take his gun with the intent to inflict great bodily harm upon the officer. Multiple eyewitnesses testified that the teenager had been rushing the officer at the time of the fatal shooting. Many Americans agreed that the officer had acted in self-defense.

However, many other Americans believed justice called for the police officer's punishment. They refused to accept the accounts of the eyewitnesses who said that the young man had been rushing the police officer and instead believed witnesses who said that he had had his hands up in surrender and had been mercilessly executed by the police officer. It's difficult to know what the truth is, but the only prudent course of action in such a case is to abide by the rule of law and have the matter settled in court, not by riots.

Historically, justice was defined by mob rule or by monarchical decrees. The founders of our nation had seen the results of this kind of "justice." They wanted nothing to do with it and wanted to craft a legal system that would be consistent regardless of who was in power. They set up our Constitution to "establish Justice" and "insure domestic Tranquility." Today we can uphold those aims by sticking to proper legal procedures, insisting that our law enforcement keep the people's best interests in mind, applying the definition of marriage consistently instead of changing its meaning, and strengthening local government.

PROPER PROCEDURE

Justice can be perverted, even in the best of systems. However, it's always best to address that injustice through the proper channels. It is true that slavery ended only through the bloodshed of the Civil War, but that tragic event became necessary only because Americans had not been diligent in addressing the evil of slavery properly. Since then, through the use of the system created by the Constitution, skillful jurists like Thurgood Marshall, who worked with the NAACP, were able to overcome the evils of Jim Crow and its segregation. If there is injustice in our country today, we should follow Marshall's example of persistent and legal pursuit of justice. If we try to take matters into our own hands, we run the risk of deluding ourselves and becoming the tyrants once we get our way.

The signers of the Constitution wanted a nation where people were treated equally regardless of their social status or ethnic origin. This could be achieved only if the leaders of the nation were willing to apply the laws equally to everyone and not pick and choose which laws they wanted to enforce. In recent decades we have seen significant deviation regarding the equal application of the laws, but again, it is not too late to rectify the situation if we the people of the United States take enough interest in our political situation to exercise our right as voters and put people in office who will uphold our Constitution.

TRUSTWORTHY LAW ENFORCEMENT

Since the beginning of human history, men have been involved in wars and tremendous strife. It appears to be a part of the human condition. The founders understood that war would never be eliminated entirely, but they felt that we could maintain peace within our own borders. If they could form a nation where the people trusted the government to uphold justice, they believed, people would be much more likely to remain peaceful.

A key ingredient for upholding justice and keeping the peace is a well-trained police force under the control of a local government elected by the people. People tend to be much more comfortable with the forces of law and order when the lawmakers are from their own area and the enforcers are people who understand local culture. This is the reason why we have local law-enforcement agencies rather than a national military presence to maintain domestic order.

Ensuring justice is a vital element of ensuring domestic tranquillity, because people who feel that they are being treated fairly are much more likely to be tranquil. A combination of fair laws and friendly and understanding agents of enforcement has a much higher chance of achieving peace and harmony than does dictatorial imposition of power.

As an elementary school pupil in Detroit, I saw the benefits of kindness and reason in authority figures. Like most of the other students, I rode the bus home from school at the end of the day. Some of the bus drivers were mean and seemed to take no interest in the children. Our bus driver, Pat, was kind and knew all the children by their names. He could frequently be seen comforting children who were distressed for one reason or another. He also knew that the children were thrilled whenever he pulled past one of the other buses, giving them a chance to cheer and make faces at the kids on the other bus. Although Pat didn't speed, he was very good at anticipating the traffic signals, which made for many exciting rides home. Because Pat developed camaraderie with the students, he was regarded very differently from the other bus drivers, who seemed much more interested in exercising authority. Some of them felt that Pat was wrong to become friendly with the kids, but what they didn't know was that the kids had the utmost respect for Pat: He never had any trouble on his bus. The kids saw him not only as an authority figure but also as a friend.

Local police forces could learn a lot from this story. If the people in a neighborhood regularly have friendly encounters with the police, their children's first impressions of officers will be as friends rather than enemies. Some police departments have developed athletic leagues and other mechanisms to foster relationships between the community and the police in an amicable way. There are far fewer problems when this is the case.

Fortunately, our country was designed in a way that allows the people to choose the type of leadership that they prefer. When we see government authorities abusing their power, we have the power to fire them. That power does not come through rioting. It comes through voting.

JUSTICE AND TRANQUILLITY IN MARRIAGE

One of the most significant changes to our Constitution involved the emancipation of the slaves and the establishment of their rights as full citizens of the United States. The important civil rights amendments added to our Constitution are critical to the protection of justice and domestic tranquillity. However, it is essential that we do not misapply the amendments and so sabotage one of the mainstays of tranquillity: marriage.

I would be a vociferous opponent of anyone who was unwilling to apply our civil rights laws equally to all American citizens. Some would argue that my opposition to gay marriage is inconsistent with that statement. I would argue that marriage was established as a religious ceremony that officially recognizes the establishment of a family and creates an ideal environment for the raising of children. It also confers upon the man and woman civil privileges such as hospital visitation and property transfer rights. I am not in favor of keeping from anyone the benefits of marriage; I just do not want to change the definition.

There is nothing in our Constitution that prevents any two consenting adults from establishing legal civil relationships that would allow them hospital visitation rights, property transfer rights, and a host of other civil rights. A gay couple need not be married in order to live together or love each other. But that is not marriage, at least as it is understood religiously.

The framers of our Constitution intended that these kinds of issues be handled by the states, where the input of the people could be most directly expressed. Citizens should be able to decide how they wish to handle the issue of marriage using voter referenda, and judges should not be able to overturn the decisions made by those citizens. Unless we are able to work through this issue at the state level, we risk ignoring the will of the people, misapplying the ideas of justice won by the civil rights movement, and damaging the domestic tranquillity created by solid marriages.

LOCAL RULE AS A SOURCE OF TRANQUILLITY

The issue of marriage is not the only one that should be decided at a local level. We are actually more likely to maintain justice and tranquillity if the majority of problems are dealt with locally. People are more likely to peacefully trust local authorities than federal. A local state judge is much more likely to pay attention to the will of the people than a federal judge who does not have to answer to those people. Local control means we can have states with a variety of positions, allowing people to seek happiness among others sharing their views. Our country is very large and can accommodate a wide variety of living preferences, as long as those of one person do not infringe upon the rights of others. When politicians prioritize local rule instead of trying to force the whole country to agree with them, I think the pursuit of happiness will be within the reach of a far greater portion of our populace.

PRESERVING JUSTICE

We will never achieve perfect justice on this earth. We will never have perfect peace. But the prescription for justice and domestic tranquillity provided in our Constitution is the best we will get. Following the patterns set out by the founders, let us fight injustice wherever we see it. Let us be disciplined in fighting it through the proper channels, being zealous in maintaining the peace. Let us keep our law enforcement accountable to the people, let us uphold marriage, and let us champion local rule. By doing all of these things, we give our children of every race a chance to enjoy an even more just and peaceful society than we have yet experienced.

CHAPTER 6
PROVIDE FOR THE COMMON DEFENSE

"The horse is prepared for the last day of battle, but the
victory belongs to the Lord."

Proverbs 21:31

Establishing and preserving internal peace was a top prior-
ity for the founders. Just as pressing was the matter of
defense against outsiders. Standing alone, any one state would
have stood little chance in a fight against a foreign power.
Imagine the state of New Hampshire taking on Great Britain
without the backing of the other states—defeat would have
been certain. Accordingly, the founders created a union to
"provide for the common defence." By combining their military forces and resources, the original thirteen colonies became
a formidable opponent to anyone foolish enough to risk attack-
ing them.

The founders also knew that every government system
risks corruption, and they wanted to make sure Americans
would be able to defend themselves should the nation's leaders become tyrannical. To that end, they ratified the Second
Amendment, guaranteeing the right of Americans to bear
arms. An armed populace is a powerful deterrent to tyrants

both domestically and internationally, and we must defend this liberty as part of our common defense.

Today America faces dangers at home and abroad. In the spirit of the preamble, the country must meet threats like ISIS with strength and wit. We must uphold the rights of Americans to defend themselves. And we must ensure that the government doesn't overstep its boundaries in the name of keeping us safe.

DEFENSE ABROAD

The maintenance of military forces is expensive, as George Washington quickly discovered in his efforts to resist the British. Today the cost of military readiness is huge, and there are many who wish to reduce those costs by decreasing American military presence throughout the world.

The advocates of a small military should remember, however, that strong defensive capabilities decrease the likelihood of attack. As the world becomes more complex, with threats from various places, it is imperative that we equip ourselves with a military force capable of facing multiple enemies simultaneously. This does not mean that we have to expend all of our resources on the military, but it does mean we must efficiently use resources adequate to "provide for the common defence."

Our country, as well as the rest of the world, faces an enormous threat from ISIS and other radical Islamic terrorist organizations that aspire to achieve world domination. These were the same aspirations held by the followers of Adolf Hitler in the 1930s. Our government must recognize the importance of directly and vigorously confronting these forces of evil. We must not make the mistake of avoiding necessary conflict; we did not get involved in World War I or World War II until we felt that American interests were directly threatened, and this proved to be the wrong choice, though we eventually were victorious.

If a vicious enemy that is willing to decapitate people, burn people alive, and even crucify children is allowed to grow with only minor to moderate resistance, it will only become a more formidable adversary in the future. If during this period of tepid responses to terrorist expansion the radical Islamists manage to acquire nuclear weapons, providing for the common defense will take on an entirely new different meaning. The longer we wait to eliminate the threat, the more difficult that task will become and the more dangerous the world will be for our children and grandchildren.

We must use all necessary resources to protect the lives of our people. Given the existence of enemies who have a stated goal of destroying our nation and our way of life, one way to provide for the common defense is to hide, which in our case would not be possible. A better option is to try to eliminate the threat, and the earlier the threat can be eliminated, the fewer lives will be lost in the conflict.

Unfortunately, these days our elected officials are slow to recognize the urgency of providing for the common defense. When the commander in chief has difficulty even publicly identifying the enemy, defending our people and territory is going to be exceedingly difficult. Our Constitution does not provide a mechanism to override poor defensive decisions by the president, perhaps because our founders could not imagine a situation where the people would be more desirous than the government of effective military action.

If the people are able to see the growing threat, but the government is resistant to acting, it is the right and responsibility of the people to peacefully protest and demand action. We are quite used to seeing protests against war, but a protest against an inadequate response to a threat that could destroy our nation may become one of the most difficult and important actions ever taken by the American people. I hope that before it is too late the government of the United States will realize that its duty to provide for the common defense includes the responsibility to implement a plan to thwart the goals of radical extremists who wish to destroy Western civilization. Our military forces are capable of achieving victory, especially when allowed to carry out their missions without micromanagement by government officials with little or no knowledge of military strategy. Unfortunately, our soldiers' job is made doubly complex when those government officials threaten to prosecute them if, in the opinion of some, they violate certain rules of ethical warfare. In the unrealistic world of the ivory-tower elites, war is like a game that has rules to which you must adhere regardless of what the other side is doing. Most of these people have never been in a war or associated with people who have experienced the horrors of war. If they had, they would recognize that in a war you must do whatever you have to do in order to survive. You do not have time to consider the ramifications of every move you make; time-consuming analysis can cost lives. If one of our soldiers makes an honest mistake during combat, the last thing he should have to worry about is being prosecuted by his own country. If we are to be successful in combat, we cannot have a fearful and confused fighting force.

The progressive movement will scream bloody murder

and say I wish to abolish the rules of the Geneva Conventions and all vestiges of common decency. To that I respond that we have complex brains, and we are capable of observing common decency while simultaneously having the backs of our combatants. Providing for the common defense means protecting Americans from attack—and protecting those who lay down their lives to keep us safe. We can act both forcefully and ethically, and we must act boldly.

DEFENSE AT HOME

Threats abroad are one thing, but what happens if there's a need for defense on America's shores? Our founders recognized that "we the People" could represent a significant fighting force if necessary to repel an invasion by foreign forces. They also knew that an armed population would discourage government overreach. The Second Amendment states, "A well regulated Militia, being necessary to the security of a free State, the right of the people to keep and bear Arms, shall not be infringed." The founders feared an overbearing central government might attempt to dominate the people and severely curtail their rights. This, in fact, is the primary reason that the Second Amendment was included in the Bill of Rights.

Most people in the United States would think it ludicrous to imagine our federal government trying to seize unconstitutional power and dominate the people. James Madison did not think this was so far-fetched; he said, "Enlightened statesmen will not always be at the helm."[1] He could foresee a day in America when radicals might assume power and try to impose upon America a different system of government.

His hope was that the establishment of such a different way of life would be difficult in America, because American citizens, having the right to keep and bear arms, would rebel.

The idea that an armed citizenry was necessary for maintaining democracy is an old one. In discussions about the Constitution, Noah Webster said, "Before a standing army can rule, the people must be disarmed; as they are in almost every kingdom in Europe. The supreme power in America cannot enforce unjust laws by the sword; because the whole body of the people are armed."[2] True to Webster's observation, American citizens have been armed for hundreds of years and they have been free for hundreds of years.

On the other hand, German citizens were disarmed by their government in the late 1930s, and by the mid-1940s Hitler's regime had mercilessly slaughtered six million Jews and numerous others whom they considered inferior. Through a combination of removing guns and disseminating deceitful propaganda, the Nazis were able to carry out their evil intentions with relatively little resistance. Atrocities involving the murder of millions of people were also carried out against the people of China, the USSR, Uganda, Cuba, Cambodia, and Turkey, among others, after the people had been disarmed by tyrants.

Given our long history of freedom and the history of domination and tyranny in nations where guns have been removed from the populace, we should heed Thomas Jefferson's warning: "Laws that forbid the carrying of arms . . . disarm only those who are neither inclined nor determined to commit crimes. . . . Such laws make things worse for the assaulted and better for the assailants; they serve rather to encourage than to prevent homicides, for an unarmed man may be attacked with greater confidence than an armed man."[3] Only law-abiding citizens are affected by legislation imposing gun control. The criminals really don't care what the law says, which is why they are criminals. Confiscating the guns of American citizens would violate the Constitution as well as rendering the citizenry vulnerable to criminals and tyrants.

Some will say that they see no problem with small handguns and hunting rifles, perhaps even shotguns. They are opposed to more powerful weaponry such as assault rifles and armor-penetrating ammunition. I too was a member of that camp until I fully recognized the intent of the Second Amendment, which is to protect the freedom of the people from an overly aggressive government. This means the people have a right to any type of weapon that they can legally obtain in order to protect themselves. They would be at a great disadvantage if they were attacked by an overly aggressive government and all they had to defend themselves with were minor firearms.

Freedom is not free and it must be jealously guarded and fought for every day. In his first inaugural address in 1789, George Washington said, "The preservation of the sacred fire of liberty and the destiny of the Republican model of government are justly considered as deeply, perhaps as finally, staked on the experiment entrusted to the hands of the American people."[4] The experiment President Washington was talking about was our system, which depends on the people to adhere to the Constitution and require their representatives to do the same, rather than accepting major unconstitutional edicts issued by smooth-talking politicians in the name of some higher social good. It was the eloquent C. S. Lewis who said, "Of all tyrannies, a tyranny sincerely exercised for the good of its victims may be the most oppressive."[5] In America we can count on many voices calling for various types of gun control after any massacre, especially when it involves children. This seems noble but is just the kind of thing that our founders feared.

Rather than trying to control or confiscate guns, it might be smarter to offer free, public gun-safety courses. In countries like Switzerland, every man within a certain age range is required to possess a gun and to know how to use it, and Switzerland has one of the lowest gun homicide rates in the world. It is clear that guns do not kill people by themselves. Rather, people who are determined to kill will find whatever means are available to accomplish their mission.

We can talk about gun-safety issues and ways to decrease the likelihood of insane people obtaining guns, but we can never compromise the intent of the Second Amendment to accomplish any other goal. It is the people who are the guardians of freedom, not the government. The power of the nation resides with the people and depends on their vigilance. The great Daniel Webster put it this way:

> There is no nation on earth powerful enough to accomplish our overthrow.... Our destruction, should it come at all, will be from another quarter. From the inattention of the people to the concerns of their government, from their carelessness and negligence, I must confess that I do apprehend some danger. I fear that they may place too implicit confidence in their public servants, and fail to properly scrutinize their

conduct; that in this way they may be made the dupes of designing men, and become the instruments of their own undoing.[6]

This chilling warning was written sixty-one years after the Declaration of Independence but still is relevant today.

We must be particularly wary in a hyperpartisan atmosphere of being, as Webster puts it, "dupes of designing men."[7] Those designing men will frequently take things that are matters of liberty and conscience and recast them as political issues. If the party faithful accept this politicization without appropriate analysis, liberty then becomes a partisan issue, and our freedom is at stake. This is one of the reasons why hyperpartisanship is so dangerous to the long-term viability of our nation. We must be intelligent enough to recognize the forces of division that are busily pitting against one another people who should actually be friends and join forces to solve problems. Many who are pulled into the politics of division actually do not recognize that they are dupes or, as Vladimir Lenin purportedly put it, "useful idiots." When people become well read and learn to think for themselves, they are less likely to move away from providing for the common defense.

WHEN IS DEFENSE TOO MUCH?

In the age of terrorism, many have advocated that we sacrifice our rights to privacy for the sake of providing early detection of terrorist activity. Our founders would be horrified; they were gravely concerned about sacrificing privacy for the sake of security. This is one of the reasons why the Fourth Amendment became part of the Bill of Rights.

Everyone is entitled to their private thoughts and musings without fear of exposure. Creative thinking is much more likely to occur in a setting where private documents cannot be seized arbitrarily based on the suspicions of some authoritarian figure. In this cyber age, the right to privacy is more important than ever, since hackers and the government can monitor your online activities without your knowledge. Surreptitiously tracking phone calls, purchasing activity, Web site visitation history, and a host of other activities is tantamount to the illegal search and seizure forbidden by the Fourth Amendment.

The government consistently denied its involvement in such activities until it was exposed by an informant. Attempts were made to excuse such invasions of privacy by emphasizing their importance in monitoring potential terrorist activities and thereby keeping all of us safe. That might be a legitimate rationale, but it should be remembered that government authorities can easily obtain a court order on a moment's notice, even in the middle of the night, when legitimate concerns are presented to the appropriate judicial authorities. Once again it will be up to "we the People" to put an end to such practices by raising our voices and utilizing the ballot box in an educated fashion.

PROTECTING OUR FUTURE

The specific threats against America's existence have changed since the founders wrote the preamble, but the enemies of liberty remain the same. As we take America forward, a strong military is still necessary for defense against threats from abroad. Human nature has not changed, so we still need an armed citizenry to defend against tyranny at home. And we should never forget that this defense is a defense of *liberty*— any actions that claim to improve safety while destroying our freedoms should be rejected. Because we have been vigilant on these fronts, our union still exists today. Let's be sure to maintain our defenses for the sake of our children tomorrow. If our common defense allows them to live in peace, they will be even more able to cultivate the "general Welfare" of our citizens, which was the next goal of the founders.

CHAPTER 7
PROMOTE THE GENERAL WELFARE

*"Do not withhold good from those who deserve it when
it's in your power to help them."*

Proverbs 3:27

L ooking out for the good of others is one of the basic ide-
als that characterizes American society. Neighbors help
neighbors. We do our best to enhance the prosperity, health,
and happiness of others in our communities. Essentially, as
private citizens we "promote the general Welfare" of our neigh-
borhoods.

According to our Constitution, our government is also to
promote the general welfare, but the avenues appropriate
for government assistance are slightly different from those
appropriate for private citizens. For one thing, it is fine for
individuals to help only those individuals closest to them—
we should all do the best we can to serve everyone, but
our means are limited, and we sometimes have to prioritize.
The federal government, on the other hand, must look out
for everyone—the *general* welfare—not just an elite few or
the members of a particular party. As private citizens, we
can and should give to those in need, and we are free to
give with no strings attached. The government, though,

shouldn't just dole out support in a way that increases dependency—it is to *promote* the welfare, not secure it. The government should use every constitutional means to improve the situation of all Americans, caring about truly public issues such as the environment and monetary policy, but it is ultimately the responsibility of the people to maintain their own welfare.

THE GENERAL WELFARE—NOT SPECIAL ACCOMMODATION

Whenever the government chooses one particular group of people to help, we end up with injustice. The laws and policies of our government should be good for all of the people, and we should not choose favorite groups for the receipt of special favors, whether those favors are monetary or legislative. The founders of our country would be horrified if they could see the influence of special-interest groups upon the legislative process in our nation's capital. So many groups receive handouts or preferential treatment in return for campaign contributions or political influence that it becomes difficult for legislators to discern the difference between what is good for their constituents and what is good for the interest group. As a result, our legislation is bloated with unnecessary pages accommodating special interests.

Many special-interest groups do need accommodation, but their needs should be balanced with the needs of the rest of Americans. This is a concept easily understood in the medical field. Most neurosurgeons wisely focus their careers on remedying the most common problems. Extraordinary cases may arise, but it makes more sense to refer those cases to experts than for all neurosurgeons to try to be prepared for all types of cases. Trying to be an expert in everything results in shallow knowledge and less expertise in every area.

I saw this firsthand in 1987 when I was privileged to lead a medical team in an unusual procedure: an attempt to separate conjoined twins from West Germany. The two were joined at the backs of their heads, and no twins joined in that manner had ever before been separated and both survived. The involved operation required seventy members and twenty-two hours of surgery. The teamwork was impressive and both twins survived. Ten years later I was called upon to lead a team in South Africa in an attempt to separate twins joined at the top of the head. There had been thirteen previous attempts to separate such twins without great success. The conditions were not optimal, but the twenty-eight-hour surgery yielded two neurologically intact boys who will soon be graduating high school.

Because I have expertise in this field, I have been involved in a number of other craniopagus surgeries, though fortunately such medical anomalies are extremely rare. The overwhelming majority of neurosurgeons will never see one in their entire career. For this reason, a great deal of attention is not devoted to studying these kinds of patients. It is not that people are uncaring but rather that practicality dictates a more judicious use of time. It makes a great deal more sense to devote one's time and resources to the things that are commonly encountered, leaving the care of the extraordinarily rare conditions to a few experts.

This commonsense principle should be applied to legislative matters involving the general population. Laws and regulations should be designed to address normal situations, while providing special mechanisms for the creation of exceptions in abnormal situations. Changing the law governing the normal situation in order to accommodate the abnormal situation is like requiring that car seats be designed to accommodate conjoined twins as well as anatomically normal children. The more sensible thing would be to require car seats to accommodate typical children and design special car seats for atypical children as needed.

This principle can be applied to a host of situations in our nation. For example, most people are heterosexual, and changing the definition of marriage to suit those outside that definition is unnecessarily complicated. Instead, we should find other ways to accommodate those needing civil unions. If we adhere to common sense, those outside the norm will not feel that they have to change things for everyone else in order to get fair treatment for themselves, and we will experience more tranquillity and tolerance on all sides. The welfare of everyone will be improved.

THE GENERAL WELFARE—NOT JUST OF ONE PARTY

Partisanship is a huge obstacle to fairness. The founders could scarcely have dreamed how bitter the rancor of the eventual two-party system would become. At the time that the Constitution was written, American political parties were in their embryonic stage. Most political figures were focused on what was good for the nation rather than what was good for their political constituency. Unfortunately, that did not last.

Shrewd politicians realized that by making their ideas into an identity with a party label, they could consistently attract voters who were not paying attention to specific issues. Today party politics have reached the point where many people consider allegiance to their party more important than allegiance to the nation. This is a dangerous trend, and in order to rectify it we will need strong leaders who are not hyperpartisan but are looking out for the good of everyone.

These leaders must be statesmen rather than politicians. Politicians tend to do things that will get them reelected and promote their ideological notions. Some politicians actually do care about their constituencies and try to live by a code of ethics, but most seem to be motivated primarily by their desire to win elections. Statesmen are wise people who express their ideas in ways the people can understand. They are unconcerned with reelection but very concerned about carrying out the will of their constituents and doing what is right for the country. Only statesmen have the courage to risk alienating their parties in order to do what is right for everyone. Only statesmen really serve the general welfare, and they do so by making sure that the laws apply equally to all citizens.

THE DANGERS OF UNFAIR TAXATION

When the founders wrote that the government should promote the general welfare, they didn't mean that the government should take money from one group to support another group. It will be difficult for us to ever achieve a sense of fairness in America as long as taxes are levied in different ways for different groups of people. The sense of injustice can poison relationships and create animosity where none should exist.

I can still remember vividly the heartache and bitterness I felt as a child when I was treated unfairly by teachers. When I was in third grade, my teacher made me sit under her desk like a dog for the whole afternoon because of a minor infraction.

When I was in fourth grade, a male teacher paddled me because a female student, who was the teacher's pet, told a lie about me because she knew that the teacher would take her side without question. Although I have long since forgiven those teachers and try not to hold grudges, I remember that the feeling of injustice was more unpleasant than the actual punishment in both cases. Similarly, when people feel abused by a system of taxation that affords favors to some while punishing others, the resentment breeds class warfare.

No group of American citizens should be singled out for extra taxation and no group should be spared taxation on the federal level. A flat tax may be the only tax that truly treats everyone fairly and thus promotes the general welfare. Under a flat tax, each citizen pays the same percentage, and there is no danger of the government favoring one group over another. An added bonus of the flat tax is that it makes politicians think twice before raising it. If raising taxes means that everybody suffers the same proportional increase, raising taxes will upset everybody, not just a small group of people. These angry voters will make their voices heard and vote the responsible politicians out of office.

Another way to make sure taxes treat everyone fairly is to close all the loopholes in the tax code. When accounting tricks let some people avoid paying taxes, unfairness automatically enters the system. A fair tax code will not overtax, but it also will not provide tax shelters or tax reductions to anyone.

Taxation is a topic where multiple opinions vie, with everyone quite convinced of the validity of their solution. A proportional income-tax system with no loopholes is the only way to avoid injecting personal biases into the argument. A proportional income-tax system also allows the rate to be set quite easily at whatever level is necessary to sustain government functions. Depending on the needs of the nation, legislators would be able to raise and lower taxes in order to best serve all citizens.

THE DANGERS OF GOVERNMENT DEPENDENCY

Promoting the general welfare does mean that the government should do things that enhance the lives of its citizens. The government should build and maintain infrastructure that supports population growth, business, and self-improvement endeavors. It should not, however, meddle in the affairs of all the citizens or control every aspect of their lives, as is done in many communist and socialist countries.

There are those who think that the government should be responsible for the well-being and basic needs of all of its citizens. There is nothing in the Constitution that imposes such a responsibility on the federal government. In fact, this attitude is harmful. A culture of dependency can rapidly develop when people are provided with things rather than with opportunities. We all have acquaintances or relatives who continually want to borrow money from us, and if we allow it, the requests are never ending and the money is almost never repaid. After a while, most people stop making such loans, recognizing that they are enabling undesirable and self-destructive behavior. In my opinion, promotion of the general welfare includes creating an environment conducive to the expansion of the number of good jobs. It means creating opportunities for advancement and enhancing the ability of citizens to care for their families. It does not mean doing things that promote dependency.

I know something of government dependency. I grew up in a single-parent home with a mother who had been able to attain only a third-grade education and who was functionally illiterate. She worked multiple jobs in order to maintain her self-sufficiency, although she occasionally did accept some public aid. She did not think that receiving public assistance was a good thing, and she constantly drilled into both my brother and me the need to work hard and to become self-sufficient citizens. Fortunately, we were able to achieve that goal and to provide a comfortable life for her in her old age. I believe she understood, even with her limited education, that if her children achieved great success, not only would they be happier but she too would end up in a much better place. By the same token, when our government concentrates on providing opportunities for self-support rather than handouts, in the long run it will have many more productive citizens. These citizens will strengthen the fabric of the country and provide an economic base that is much more capable of promoting the general welfare than handouts are.

In the late 1960s the idea of creating general welfare programs for the people became popular. Since that time, we as a nation have spent several trillion dollars on general welfare programs. One would think that such a high level of expenditure would ensure success. It would not be unreasonable to believe that today there would be fewer people on food stamps, fewer single-parent homes, fewer people involved in the penal system, and less poverty in general. None of these problems have decreased, though. There is no need to demonize those who have been responsible for this tremendous waste of resources, but we can hope that they too have the ability to objectively analyze the results of such spending and join in the effort to truly improve the lives of all Americans.

PROMOTING PRIVATE CHARITY

We can endlessly analyze and dissect the reasons for increasing poverty in the United States, but the pertinent question is "What can we do about it?" Is dealing with poverty the responsibility of the federal government? No, it is not. However, the government does have a responsibility to promote the general welfare, so the question becomes "What does that mean?"

I believe the best way for the government to improve the lives of its citizens is to encourage the establishment of compassionate programs by business, industry, Wall Street, churches, and community groups. Not only is there tremendous wealth associated with all of the aforementioned groups but, more important, they have members in virtually every city and town in America, which means they can develop personal relationships with those in need.

Governmental programs are often faceless and unsustainable. Handouts create more dependency in the populace, decreasing overall societal productivity and depleting the resources of the agencies providing the handouts. The taxpayer base decreases, the dependent population increases, and taxpayer money runs out. Historically, when governments have taken on the responsibility of social warfare from the cradle to the grave, societies have ended up with a small group of elites at the top who own and control everything, a rapidly vanishing middle class, and a greatly expanded dependent class.

By creating the right kind of programs with or without government encouragement, the private sector can empower the disadvantaged members of our society and allow them to realize the American dream. The variety of programs that could be created is almost limitless, especially in a creative society like America's.

The good news is that we the people can be very good at taking care of one another. I recently visited a facility in Las Vegas called Opportunity Village. Its goal is to provide jobs for intellectually challenged individuals, a group usually neglected by society. At Opportunity Village these individuals have an opportunity to earn a paycheck, an achievement that contributes substantially to their self-esteem and happiness. This beautiful organization is 80 percent funded by the private sector. I couldn't help but notice that not only did Opportunity Village bring joy and practical help to a needy population, but the work of helping others was immensely satisfying to its staff and volunteers. This organization's private endeavors vastly improve the quality of life of all involved.

This is just one of the many wonderful programs that exist throughout our country. When people invest their time and their money in other people within their communities, they bless their neighbors in need and improve the community as a whole. Anything the government can do to facilitate these kinds of programs, short of taking them over, will promote the general welfare.

One helpful program would be to establish dependable day-care centers, particularly in inner cities, where 73 percent of black babies are born out of wedlock. Generally with the arrival of the first baby, the mother's education ceases and the child and subsequent children are plunged into a life of dependency. Dependable day-care centers would allow that mother to get her GED, associate's degree, bachelor's degree, or perhaps a higher degree and go on to become a self-sustaining, independent member of society who can teach her children to be independent, thus helping to break the cycle of dependency and poverty.

Another community-based program that I have seen work facilitates the development of relationships between boys from disadvantaged single-parent homes and well-to-do businessmen. These men informally adopt boys who are clearly on a dangerous path of self-destruction and introduce them to the values found in traditional faith-based families. In many cases they pay for the private education of the youths in faith-based schools. Nearly 100 percent of those young men not only graduate from high school but also pursue higher education and become contributing members of society.

These kinds of programs are a double win, because the chosen children and their families benefit from a new, helpful relationship while the helping family benefits from the satisfaction of providing a hand up rather than a handout. The big winner is the nation, because every child we can prevent from going down that path of self-destruction is one less person we have to be afraid of or protect our family from, one less person we have to pay for in the penal or welfare system, and one more taxpaying, productive member of society who may discover a new energy source or the cure for cancer.

Breaking cycles of dependency, establishing cordial relationships between people of differing economic means, and reestablishing sound values and principles in our society can serve only to strengthen the fabric of our nation, which is what any government should want to do and which clearly promotes the general welfare. Of course, the progressives will ignore the facts and claim that I am advocating eliminating all governmental safety nets. They will say that now that I have "made it," I want to pull up the ladder and keep others from benefiting. This kind of nonsense is typical of the scare tactics they use to maintain support for their failed policies and prevent traction for programs that would actually help the people rather than the political ambitions of ideological politicians.

THE BENEFIT OF SUPPORTING FAMILIES

Promoting two-parent homes is another way of supporting the general welfare that infuriates progressives. As a youngster growing up in poverty, I did notice that the families around us that had both a mother and a father were financially much more prosperous. Many sociological studies today continue to show that children growing up in two-parent homes are much less likely to live in poverty. Since this is a well-established fact, governmental policies and programs should support the establishment and maintenance of two-parent homes. That would be consistent with promoting the general welfare. It would also lessen the burden on society, since there would be less poverty. This kind of thinking is anathema to the politically correct crowd, who will advocate for alternative families until their dying breath. They are totally unconcerned with the facts and cling tenaciously to their faulty ideology. I believe they would be much happier if they simply accepted the facts and were content with the existence of alternative family structures, without arguing for equivalency.

PROTECTING THE ENVIRONMENT

Though we tend to associate the term "welfare" with social safety nets, there are other government agencies that should promote the general welfare in other ways. For example, the Environmental Protection Agency (EPA) was established to protect the land, air, and waters of the United States from those who would destroy them in order to increase their profits. When functioning properly, the EPA should work in conjunction with industry and academia to discover and employ the best strategies for preserving our environment while still being able to take advantage of our abundant natural resources.

Today many people act as if we can either protect the environment or develop our resources. This is ridiculous. It is eminently possible to utilize petroleum-based resources in an environmentally friendly way while at the same time encouraging and facilitating the development of clean, renewable energy sources. Over the course of time the renewable resources will probably supplant the petroleum-based ones, which is as it should be when progress is made. Certainly there is no reason for environmentalists and energy businesses to be battling each other and becoming political enemies. We are smart and capable enough to pursue more than one goal at a time.

When governmental agencies like the EPA are used to promote ideological agendas instead of the common good, they hurt our nation. But when they behave as they should, they safeguard our resources to our benefit.

MAINTAINING OUR CURRENCY

The Treasury Department is another agency that promotes the general welfare. It is supposed to work with other agencies and financial institutions to provide a solid financial foundation for our nation. Its actions should be oriented toward protecting the value of our currency, both today and tomorrow. This department, along with Congress and the executive branch of government, must be reoriented toward decreasing the federal debt, empowering the responsible financial institutions, and fighting financial fraudulent activity. By so doing it will greatly enhance the quality of life for our children.

ULTIMATELY, THE PEOPLE ARE RESPONSIBLE

As wonderful as our government agencies are, we must never lose sight of one thing: The American people are responsible for their own welfare. There are two major systems of government that are at odds with each other in America today. Socialism puts government in the driver's seat, with the responsibility to care for the basic needs of all citizens from cradle to grave. It is a superb system for those without a great deal of ambition who simply want to be secure and minimize the risk of adversity in their lives. The other system is capitalism, which places individuals in the driver's seat, with responsibility for their own lives but also with a tremendous amount of liberty. Capitalism provides a tremendous amount of economic upside for those who are willing to work hard, take calculated risks, and be innovative.

The founders of our nation were in favor of putting individuals in charge of their lives, and their limits on government have allowed capitalism to be America's prevailing system. As a result, the general welfare has flourished. In recent years, however, there has been a movement toward much greater government involvement not only in business and industry but also in public education, energy development, health care, and many other things, including personal aspects of one's life, such as sexuality, the discipline of children, and public displays of faith. Although the founders did not intend to establish a country that was government-centric, they created a constitution that would allow the people either to accept such a fundamental change in their governance or to fortify the government against these encroachments on liberty.

The bottom line is that the people get to decide what kind of government they wish to have, but we must be forceful and brave if we are to maintain our freedoms. Two luminaries in American history were quite eloquent on this topic. Patrick Henry said, "The battle, sir, is not to the strong alone; it is to the valiant, the active, the brave."[1] President Dwight D. Eisenhower said, "History does not long entrust the care of freedom to the weak or the timid."[2] Both men seem to be saying that the American people have no one but themselves to blame if they relinquish the free and open environment that has improved the well-being of so many.

The impulse to care for others is central to the well-being of our nation. We should by no means squelch the desire to help others, and we should encourage our government to serve the general public. However, let us be wise as we move forward. We must ensure that we don't let well-meaning but misguided people increase class warfare and dependency by giving in a misguided or politically motivated way. Instead we should embrace common sense and kindness, trusting Americans to help themselves, help one another, and know the best way to improve the welfare of every citizen.

CHAPTER 8
SECURE THE BLESSINGS OF LIBERTY TO OURSELVES AND OUR POSTERITY

*"Good people leave an inheritance to their grandchil-
dren, but the sinner's wealth passes to the godly."*

Proverbs 13:22

By the time the Constitution was penned, the colonists had already gained their independence from England. Our founders were determined never to relinquish that freedom to another outside power, and they took steps to make sure their children would also defend liberty. They feared that in the future some group would decide that it had a better idea of how the country should be run and would try to impose its ideas on everyone else by inappropriate legislation or force. The Constitution was written in such a way as to make this power grab almost impossible. As long as we follow its guidelines, it will be difficult for any force, external or internal, to successfully remove American liberties.

Today the forces threatening our children are much sneakier than direct attempts to usurp power. We may not be facing a king threatening to take our liberty, but the danger is still real. Our children's freedom today is threatened by debt, ignorance, and abortion. To maintain the spirit of the Constitution, we must address these dangers before it is too late.

DEBT—A DANGER TO OUR CHILDREN

Proverbs 22:7 says, "The borrower is servant to the lender." Thomas Jefferson recognized this truth when he said that it is immoral to pass debt to the next generation.[1] Today our mounting debt is essentially guaranteeing that our children will be servants to the powers that our nation owes. Through no fault of their own, future generations will be forced to pay for our mistakes. This was not the intention of the founders. They envisioned a government that would be fiscally responsible and would empower its citizens by keeping them free of debt.

The Constitution gives Congress the right to tax the people in order to pay government debts, provide for the common defense, and promote the general welfare of the American people. The founders gave Congress a great deal of latitude when it came to what taxes would be and how they would work. Unfortunately, though this vagueness helped unite the delegates, it has been abused by our government in a way that would horrify the founders.

When the Constitution was written, there was no expectation that American citizens would one day be paying large portions of their earnings to the government. Back then the government was relatively small and relatively efficient. As its size has increased, its efficiency has decreased. The diffusion of responsibility has made it difficult to hold anyone accountable for the ballooning of a gigantic and unresponsive bureaucracy, so the government has continued to grow, forcing the American people to pay taxes to fund its expansion.

The government is now so bloated that taxation can't raise enough funds to maintain it. To obtain the money it wants, the government borrows from outside powers. The Constitution gives our government the power to borrow money without placing specific restrictions on such borrowing, precisely because our founders could never have imagined the place we are today. When the Constitution was written, our leaders presumed we would feel a sense of responsibility to repay our debts and not pass them along to the next generation. They didn't realize that we would disregard constitutional limits, expand our government, and be willing to do anything to keep the government going.

Perhaps the founders should have foreseen our irresponsibility. Examination of the histories of other pinnacle nations such as ancient Rome, Spain, France, and Great Britain demonstrates that we are not the first dominant power to experience runaway fiscal irresponsibility. We, however, have not yet been destroyed or greatly diminished by debt. There is still time to turn things around, but we must act immediately.

As I write this book, our national debt is over $18.1 trillion.[2] A mere six years ago, it was only about half that amount.[3] If we were to stop accumulating debt as a nation and instead pay down the debt at a rate of $1 billion a day, it would take fifty years to neutralize the debt. Sadly, we are not merely failing to pay down the debt but are actually increasing it at a rate of approximately $2 billion per day.[4] We know that this will adversely affect future generations, but the number is becoming so large that we could experience catastrophic results within our own lifetimes.

Because we have a representative government, the people actually bear some responsibility for our rapidly increasing national debt. The government is supposed to conform to the will of the people, so the people must make it clear to the government that they oppose the continued borrowing and spending that is ruining the future of the next generations of Americans.

This is not a Democratic or Republican issue, because if our nation becomes bankrupt, no one will be spared. Everyone has to pay the price of these enormous debts, regardless of whose fault they are. Both Democrats and Republicans have implemented reckless fiscal policies, and both parties are at fault for this risk to our children's future. It's time for voters to reject politicians of both parties who continue to jeopardize the financial future of our nation. These people must be replaced with individuals who understand how to balance a budget and reduce our debt by stimulating growth and implementing financial restraint.

Financial restraint will require sacrifices on our part, but if we care about our children, we will gladly make those sacrifices. After all, many Americans have made much bigger sacrifices for us. When Nathan Hale, who became an American spy when only twenty years old during the revolution, had been captured by the British and was preparing for execution, he famously said, "I only regret that I have but one life to lose for my country."[5] Hale was clearly thinking about those who would inhabit this great country in the future. His sacrifices were made to ensure a high quality of life for future Americans. Over the years, many of our brave soldiers have fought on foreign soil, with the full knowledge that they were unlikely to ever see their homeland or their loved ones again. Like Nathan Hale, they gave their lives to ensure freedom and a high quality of life for those of us living today.

When I was a child, we were very poor, but my mother did everything within her power to minimize the impact of poverty on our lives. She would leave our home before the crack of dawn and frequently not get back until after midnight. She would go from one job to the next, scrubbing floors, changing diapers, cleaning toilets, and doing what other people didn't want to do in order to provide for us. My mother was an attractive woman, and there was no end to the line of potential suitors promising to take care of her. She rebuffed their advances and basically sacrificed her own life in order to increase the chances that my brother and I would be successful in life. One of the greatest joys of my life was to be able to provide a comfortable retirement for her. She was able to travel the world and to pursue her hobbies without constraint. But what made her much happier than the material things my brother and I were able to provide for her later in life was the fact that her sacrifices made success possible for her sons, who were able to become contributors to society.

The adults in our society today can act selflessly, as did my mother, or they can continue to live selfishly, squandering the resources that would improve the quality of life of future generations. We must ask ourselves whether we are willing to deprive ourselves of anything in order to improve the lives of those coming after us.

EDUCATION—THE GUARDIAN OF LIBERTY

Just as it is our responsibility not to pass debt on to our children, it *is* our responsibility to pass knowledge on to them. Freedom cannot last long without education, because an uneducated populace is likely to be duped by tyrants. An educated populace cannot be easily manipulated and is the foundation of a strong society. Providing for the education of our children is a key part of ensuring that the blessings of liberty will still exist when our grandchildren are adults.

Many in our society have worked hard to try to provide a good education for the masses, but sometimes they are reluctant to actually examine the data when formulating educational policies. For example, studies show that home-schoolers often reach extremely high achievement levels, followed by those educated in private schools, charter schools, and, last, public schools. Yet education officials still tend to push public school as if it were the only right option. To me the logical position seems to be to advocate for school choice. Parents know what is best for their children, and we see hundreds of parents lining up to try to get their children into charter schools. They have seen the results and want their children to benefit. Our entire society should share this goal, because each well-educated pupil benefits our society. If parents believe and studies show that charter schools are helping our children, we should drop the politicking and increase the number of charter schools.

We also should make sure that public education provides balanced information to our children. The Department of Education was originally created to ensure that we had an educated and informed populace capable of selecting appropriate representatives to manage the country. The Department of Education would serve a useful purpose if it actually attempted to ensure the best possible education for everyone, paying special attention to those mired in poverty, because education provides the best ladder of escape. Instead, in recent decades this department has been invaded by bureaucrats who have seen fit to vastly expand its mission. This expansion has resulted in a change in the subject matter being taught, to the point of indoctrination against our own founding fathers' principles. It is important that our leaders take seriously the necessity to improve the Department of Education—if it hinders the education of our children for many more years, it will destroy the foundations of our freedom.

ABORTION—THE LITERAL ENEMY OF OUR CHILDREN

Financial stability and education will do our children no good if they are not alive to experience them. Our founders were committed to a belief in the importance of life and liberty, and we must fight to see those rights extended to our children still in the womb.

Why was life so important to the founders of our nation? Perhaps it was because they came from countries where human life was not cherished by those in power. Historically, monarchs in many cases could simply order someone executed, and the victim would have no recourse. People could be forced into servitude and the fruits of their labor confiscated, again with no recourse. On the other hand, we in the United States have typically placed a high premium on human life and gone to extraordinary lengths to save and preserve it.

There was a time in America when great celebrations surrounded the news of a pregnancy, because it was assumed that this was the beginning of a new life. Pregnancy represented continuity of a family legacy and continuation of the species, not to mention a new citizen for our young nation. In our more recent history, we have fallen away from standing up for life.

Now many in our society want to redefine the beginning of life and allow the termination of fetal human beings who have no recourse. The head of the American Civil Liberties Union (ACLU) once told me that it was his belief that a woman had a right to kill a baby until the second it was born. As you know, the ACLU claims to speak for those who cannot speak for themselves. I would think that that would include fully formed babies that have not yet been born but are hours away from a normal live birth.

Since life was such an important issue for the founders of our nation, it might be worthwhile to invest more thought in the subject of when it begins. Many of the same people who gladly sanction abortion on demand go to great lengths to preserve the habitats of endangered creatures that are considerably less sophisticated than a nineteen-week-old human fetus. And a fetus even younger than that can react to environmental stimuli and has a brain that is developing at a rate of 400 million neurons per day. Within a couple of months of conception, a fetus already has well-developed fingers and toes, as well as facial features and a body that is distinctly human. Although some will continue to insist that this represents nothing more than a meaningless clump of cells, few can stand to look at a video of an abortion where the head is ripped off and the body dismembered.

Abortion always has been and probably always will be an emotional issue. The Supreme Court of the United States tried to put it to rest with its 1973 ruling on the case of *Roe v. Wade*, using section 1 of the Fourteenth Amendment, which says, "No State shall make or enforce any law which shall abridge the privileges or immunities of citizens of the United States; nor shall any State deprive any person of life, liberty, or property without due process of law; nor deny to any person within its jurisdiction the equal protection of the laws." This so-called due process clause of the amendment was interpreted by the Supreme Court to mean that a woman's right to have an abortion and to privacy was protected. From another perspective it could have been argued that the right of the fetus to live was protected by the same clause.

Currently the Supreme Court has ruled that the fetus is a living human being if it is capable of survival outside of the womb, even with medical support. The age at which this viability test precludes abortion is a moving target as advances in neonatal medicine take place.

Judicial rulings are highly subjective and depend largely on the political makeup of the court. This may seem unfair to those who do not like or agree with the rulings, but over the course of time the thrust of the various rulings seems to even out because the makeup of the court tends to change. There is hope that the Supreme Court may one day rule differently on abortion, but it would make more sense for the Court to allow states to decide the matter for themselves.

One of the real beauties of having fifty different state governments is that almost everyone can find a place of happiness where the people believe as they do. Ultimately, it would make a great deal of sense to allow the people of each state to vote on the issue after they have been objectively educated. Obviously, for this to work, it would have to be difficult or almost impossible for judges to overrule the will of the people.

In the meantime we must recognize that the lives of real children are at stake. No ruling that allows the killing of children can be in line with the Constitution's stated purpose of "secur[ing] the Blessings of Liberty to ourselves and our Posterity."

TAKING ACTION

Do the people have any recourse, or must we simply sit idly by and watch the financial future, education, and very lives of our children be destroyed? Millions of Americans are so disgusted that they have simply tuned out and reconciled themselves to the idea that there is no difference between the political parties, that everyone is in it for themselves, and that no one really cares about the people or the future. In the past they might have been right, but in recent years groups of citizen activists have become more vocal and less intimidated by name-calling and bad press. More and more people representing these courageous Americans have been elected to Congress or are finding other ways of influencing the country.

We have just touched on a few of the problems that face American society today. They all have one thing in common: They can be solved when "we the People" manifest the courage, knowledge, and fortitude to impose our will upon the government and change it according to our vision for American society. We cannot let self-important bureaucrats ruin our children's future. We the people are at the pinnacle of the power structure for a very good reason, and we should be grateful to God, who inspired the framers of our Constitution to provide a mechanism for determining our own destiny. We have benefited from the ideas presented in the preamble, and it is our God-given responsibility to see that those ideas benefit future generations too.

THE CONSTITUTION ITSELF

Thus far we have examined the purposes behind the Constitution. We've discovered its foundational ideas and have discussed ways to apply those principles to today's governance. Now that we have this understanding of the Constitution's "heart," it's time to examine the structure and language that are its "bones."

In the seven articles making up the Constitution, the founders set up a government that has three separate branches, each with distinct duties and powers. Each branch is meant to rein in the other two when they do anything unfair or poorly thought through. This is what is meant by a "system of checks and balances."

The first branch, the legislative, consists of the United States House of Representatives and the United States Senate; this branch writes the laws of the United States. The executive branch, which consists of the president of the United States, the vice president of the United States, the Executive Office of the President, and all of the cabinet departments, is tasked with enforcing those laws. The judicial branch, which consists of the United States Supreme Court and the federal courts as designated by Congress, has the responsibility of administering justice through a court system.

Our Constitution also defines the kinds of laws that may be created, the process that the legislative branch of our government must follow in creating such laws, and the methods to be used for their enforcement. It further delineates those powers that are specifically granted to the federal government and says that all other powers are retained by the states or the people.

Our Constitution has been in effect for well over two hundred years. It served us superbly when we were relatively small and inconsequential, and it serves us just as well now that we are the most powerful nation in the world. This says a great deal about its versatility and relevance in all situations. In this section we will examine the entire document article by article, seeking to discover its wisdom and learning how to defend it.

In most cases I will talk about the specific provisions in my own words. The full text of the Constitution can be found in this book's appendix, and I encourage all readers to read it for themselves.

CHAPTER 9

ARTICLE 1, THE LEGISLATIVE BRANCH

*"Everyone must submit to governing authorities. For all
authority comes from God, and those in positions of
authority have been placed there by God."*

Romans 13:1

In my spare time I love to play pool. I find it relaxing and challenging after a long and stressful day, and I enjoy playing it with my wife, who has become a formidable opponent. Whenever I am playing at a location away from home or playing a new challenger at home, the game begins with a statement of the house rules. There are rules about these rules: They must be mutually agreed upon before the game starts, they cannot be changed midgame, and outsiders have no right to change them.

The first article of the Constitution establishes the rules for the branch of our government that writes our laws. It tells us who can make the laws, sets in place the procedures for writing them, and tells us their scope and limits. Without these guidelines the functioning of government would be confusing and dangerous, because the most powerful factions would be able to force their will upon the people.

Known as the legislative branch, Congress is made up of

two houses, the Senate and the House of Representatives. Always remember that your senators and representatives are representatives of the people. Your involvement is essential to making sure that they are an accurate reflection of the people's will. Through your vote you give power to your fellow citizens to make the laws of our nation, so it is your responsibility to choose wisely.

ALL LEGISLATIVE POWERS

The first section of the first article establishes one key principle for American government: Only our elected legislators can make laws. Congress, and only Congress, has the power to create laws. The reason for restricting legislative power to Congress is simple—of all the members of our federal government, the representatives are the closest to the people. The founders wanted to make sure that the people were truly in charge of lawmaking, but they knew true democracy was impractical—imagine having millions of people voting on each issue Congress takes up. Instead they set up a democratic republic, where the people's elected representatives make decisions on behalf of their fellow citizens. This system, when it works correctly, is both efficient and responsive to the needs of the people.

Our laws are not to be made or remade by the president or by the courts or by anyone else. The president or judges may make suggestions to Congress, and there are situations when the other two branches can rein in the legislative branch, but they have no legal power to write laws.

Unfortunately, both the judicial and executive branches

keep ignoring this fundamental principle. In 2012 the Supreme Court actually changed the Affordable Care Act in order to make it constitutional. President Obama, through the use of executive orders, has altered the nation's immigration policies. Executive orders are constitutional, but they are meant to be used only rarely and in circumstances where such quick action is required that congressional action is not feasible. In this case the immigration issue was not an emergency, and the president used the order to make a political point.

These recent unconstitutional actions should alarm every student of our founding document. We should encourage the courts to strike down illegal executive orders. And we should pay close attention to which players are disregarding the rule of law and vote them—or, in the case of judges, their supporters—out of office at the first opportunity.

THE HOUSE OF REPRESENTATIVES

During the Constitutional Convention of 1787, the representatives of the large and small states fought bitterly over how representation would work. The large states argued that they deserved more representatives in the federal government because they had more people. The small states argued that each state should have equal representation so that the large states could not force unfair policies on the small states.[1]

Fortunately, the parties were eventually able to arrive at a satisfactory compromise. Every state has two senators, which gives all states equal power in the Senate. The number of representatives each state has in the House of Representatives is proportionate to the state's population, which gives the large states more power in that body of Congress. Currently we have 535 members of Congress, 100 of whom are in the Senate and 435 of whom are in the House of Representatives.

Section 2 of Article 1 outlines the structure of the House of Representatives. It mandates that each state have elected representatives in proportion to its population, requires that those representatives be elected every two years, and sets rules for who can vote and how the population of each state is calculated.

Term Duration and Limits

The founders of our country wanted the representatives of the people to be accountable to the people, so they chose to require elections or reelections every other year. They felt that this frequency would keep the representatives closely connected to their constituents because two years was too short a time to forget about where they came from.

The shortness of the term was also designed to make being a representative possible for more people. Being a representative was initially a tough job with very few perks, so most people would not have been interested in serving for very long. Today being a U.S. representative is a prestigious and well-compensated position, so this is less of a concern.

Many representatives now run for office multiple times, and they tend to become more corrupt with each term. They need to raise cash to finance their repeated campaigns and as a result become entangled with special-interest groups. Ideally, informed voters would recognize cronyism and vote corrupt politicians out of office. However, because apathy and lack of education seem to prevent this from happening, it may be appropriate to consider a constitutional amendment establishing term limits.

Eligibility

Who is eligible to be elected to the House of Representatives? The founders decided that representatives must be at least twenty-five years old, residents of the state they represented, and citizens of the United States for at least seven years prior to their election. This would ensure that representatives were mature enough to lead and familiar enough with their constituents to represent them well.

Election Procedure

Initially the founders were unsure of who should be allowed to vote for the U.S. representatives. They resolved the dilemma by allowing each state to determine its own voter qualifications, requiring only that each state use the same qualifications that it used for electing representatives to its largest publicly elected state legislative body.

Determining Number of Representatives

For a system based on population to work correctly, an accurate count of the population of each state must be conducted on a regular basis. Because the count had to be done meticulously, the crafters of the Constitution decided that a census must be done once every ten years. We still use that timetable today.

Because the number of representatives was tied to population, states that had many slaves, indentured servants, and in some cases Native Americans wanted to count these people in the censuses, even though they were not voters. The slave states were particularly eager for power in order to create legislation that would allow for the expansion of slavery throughout the entire nation. In an effort to dilute the power of the slave states, the Northern delegates secured a compromise. A slave would count as three fifths of a person, not because the founders thought slaves were not fully human but because counting them that way gave the abolitionists a fighting chance of ending the evil practice.

An extraordinary amount of trust must be placed in the census system, because any state could gain unfair advantages by inflating the number of its population. There already exist a number of safeguards to preclude cheating, but further measures are constantly being evaluated and should be welcomed. I hope we can continue to find ways to encourage integrity in all aspects of government operations.

Originally each U.S. representative was to represent no more than thirty thousand people, but as our nation grew this became impractical. With that ratio there would be an unworkably large number of legislators in the House of Representatives. For this reason, in 1929 a law was passed limiting the total number of representatives to 435, which is where it remains today.

Vacancies and Leadership

Whenever a House seat is vacated midterm (because of death, resignation, or anything else), the Constitution requires the governor of the representative's state to order a special election to fill the seat. This is an important clause because it prevents any state governor from appointing U.S. representatives instead of having them elected by the people.

The most powerful person in the House is the Speaker of the House. The Speaker is chairman of all the official meetings of the House of Representatives and has the ability to promote a bill—or to suppress it, even though many other representatives have invested enormous time, effort, and resources in it. The members of the House of Representatives can choose anyone they want to be the Speaker of the House, whether that person is an elected representative or not. If the members of the House were inspired by a judge, a CEO of a corporation, a college professor, or a housewife, they could legally choose that individual to be Speaker of the House. However, the position almost always goes to a representative who is a member of the majority party in the House.

Impeachment

Finally, section 2 of Article 1 states that the House of Representatives is the sole holder of the power to impeach public officials of the U.S. government. Obviously, a transgression would have to be fairly substantial to prompt initiation of impeachment proceedings. Such violations of the public trust might include treason, bribery, and other acts that are illegal or generally regarded as morally corrupt. In an impeachment proceeding the House acts like a prosecuting attorney, presenting the case to the Senate, which then acts as judge and jury. Unless the Senate agrees with the House on the impeachment, the accused individual cannot be forcibly removed from office.

Fortunately, impeachment proceedings are few and far

between, and the bar is set so high that they are seldom mentioned in the corridors of power in Washington. Nevertheless, it is comforting to know that our Constitution contains built-in protections against dishonesty and criminal activity by government officials.

Room for Reform

Although the founders did an excellent job of defining the roles of all the branches of government, including the House of Representatives, today this congressional body has great difficulty getting things done. The repeated gerrymandering of voting districts has resulted in a situation where the vast majority of congressional seats are "safe." The district lines have been drawn in such a way that the majority of the voting population in each district belongs to a single party. As a result, extreme candidates from both parties tend to win elections. They have a hard time compromising on issues that affect the entire population, contributing to congressional gridlock. In order to preserve our freedom, it may be necessary to resolve these problems by amending the Constitution to enact term limits and eliminate the practice of gerrymandering.

THE SENATE

Section 3 of Article 1 sets up the rules of the Senate. By allocating each state two senators, the founders equalized the power of small and large states to a significant degree. Every state, regardless of its size, would have two senatorial representatives to protect its interests. A coalition of small states would be a powerful opponent of legislation that would benefit only large states and put small states at a disadvantage.

Election Procedure

As the Constitution originally designed the Senate, senators were elected by state legislatures. The Seventeenth Amendment, enacted in 1913, changed that arrangement and mandated direct election of United States senators. Without question, states through their legislatures were more powerful under the old system, but corruption and manipulation were also easier. Many felt that direct election was a more democratic process than allowing state legislators to send their chosen representatives to the Senate.

Eligibility

Unlike representatives, who are elected every two years, senators are elected every six. But rather than having all senators up for election at the same time, the Constitution staggers senators' elections so that one third of Senate seats are open for election every two years. Because the other two thirds of the senators remain, a sense of institutional memory and stability is provided. The frequent elections keep the senators close to the voters, but the staggering means that the business of the Senate does not have to restart every two years.

The standards for senators are a little bit higher than those for representatives: "No Person shall be a Senator who shall not have attained to the Age of thirty Years, and been nine Years a Citizen of the United States, and who shall not, when elected, be an Inhabitant of that State for which he shall be chosen." Senators must have at least five years' more life experience than representatives. Since they each have more power and serve longer, it makes sense that the senators are screened more rigorously. Currently the majority of people entering the Senate have already experienced success in some other career and have a good sense of how things work in the business, social, and international arenas. Whether they possess wisdom is another matter. It is up to the voters to determine whether candidates for the Senate have both sufficient knowledge and integrity to represent them well.

Leadership

The only duty assigned to the vice president of the United States by the Constitution is that of president of the Senate. The vice president learns about all the bills and laws that are being considered and is aware of all official governmental personnel appointments and nominations for congressional approval. The vice president also hears about treaties with other nations and war efforts. When there is a vote in the Senate, the vice president does not cast a vote unless there is a tie, in which case he or she casts the deciding vote.

If for some reason the vice president is not available, senatorial business can still be carried out, with the Senate's president pro tempore (temporary president) acting in place of the vice president. As a long-standing tradition, the most senior senator in the majority party has generally been elected president pro tem.

Impeachment

While the House can initiate impeachment trials, only the Senate has the power to try and convict in those trials. Unless two thirds of the senators vote for conviction, the accused party is counted innocent. The founders did not want impeachment of the president to be an easy thing, because they fully recognized that partisan politics would likely come into play and the desire for revenge would virtually bring the government to a halt every few years.

The most recent high-profile impeachment trial in the United States involved President William Jefferson Clinton, who was charged with perjury and obstruction of justice in cases involving alleged infidelity with two different women. The House voted to impeach President Clinton almost strictly along party lines, but the requirement of a two-thirds vote by the Senate was a high bar and was not met. The wisdom of the Constitution kept a politically motivated charge from being upheld.

The Constitution makes it clear that impeachment can't result in anything more than removal from office. The Senate can punish officials only by removing them from office and denying them positions of honor in any other branch of the federal government. It would clearly be inappropriate and unconstitutional to inflict further significant punishment without an official trial by one's peers, though the convicted government official is still subject to a subsequent trial in the same court system that tries and exonerates or punishes all American citizens.

ELECTIONS AND CONGRESSIONAL SESSIONS

As mandated by section 4 of Article 1, congressional elections are held on the same day across the nation. The regulations regarding those elections are left in the hands of the states, but Congress has the duty of ensuring that they are fair and honest.

To decrease intimidation, Congress mandates that secret ballots be used and that certain forms of identification be required in most states in order to vote.

In recent years some political entities have argued that requiring voter identification is racist, because people in certain ethnic groups have a difficult time obtaining the appropriate identification. However, in virtually all countries of the world, voter identification is required. And in many of those countries the population is quite uniform, so racism doesn't seem to be the motivation there. I hope that the energy that is expended complaining that voter-identification laws aren't fair can be harnessed for good and used to get people registered and equipped with appropriate identification well before elections occur.

Because kings of England had tried to suppress Parliament, section 4 of Article 1 requires that Congress assemble at least once per year. By prescribing at least one annual meeting, the founders guaranteed that Congress would meet to conduct business, regardless of who held power in the executive branch of government. The Constitution also gives the president the power to convene special sessions of Congress as necessary. There is no designated length of time for a congressional session, which means a single session can last for several months if necessary.

CONGRESSIONAL ORDER

Our founders recognized that our representatives would be human beings with human failings. They knew that we would always have flawed leaders, so they set in place procedural rules to mitigate those leaders' failings. By setting in place plans for discipline, attendance, appropriate punishment, and adequate compensation, the framers did the best they could to protect the people's interests.

In sections 5 and 6 of Article 1, the Constitution outlines the rules of congressional procedure. First of all, Congress has the power to deny a seat to anyone elected in a dishonest way or who they feel is not worthy to occupy a seat. Without this ability, unsavory characters would contrive all kinds of nefarious plans to capture a seat. Fortunately, a two-thirds majority vote is all that is needed to keep an undesirable person from becoming a member of Congress.

The rules of attendance are simple. A majority or quorum of members of each house is necessary to do business. In practice, smaller numbers than a quorum frequently conduct the business of Congress, as long as none of the members present objects. Congress is also given the power to compel members to attend sessions and perform the duties for which they have been elected.

Both houses are to maintain discipline, keep records of their proceedings, and coordinate their actions when in session. It is also important to be able to document the activities of congressional members as they carry out their sworn duties. Many people are familiar with the *Congressional Record*, which records the activities of Congress so that they can be studied by the public. Additionally, the Senate has the *Senate Journal*, and the House has the *House Journal*. These records can be obtained online.

In order to protect the freedom of the legislators, the Constitution declares that they may not be tried for anything they say—barring treason, felony, or breach of peace. This kind of freedom allows them to openly express their opinions without fear of arrest or litigation. Of course, if they are guilty of egregious acts, they will not be protected.

Our legislators also are to be paid, since they must refrain from holding other government jobs while in office. This requirement ensures that senators and representatives will not be distracted by other government jobs. It further prevents them from creating highly paid jobs for themselves at the expense of the taxpayers.

PASSING BILLS

While the rules for legislative procedures set out in section 7 of Article 1 are not many, they are extremely important, and when they are violated, the people suffer. As an example, the only people with the ability to introduce tax bills are members of the House of Representatives. Fortunately, they are elected every other year, which means that the people have an opportunity to monitor their taxing activities and reelect or reject them accordingly. The people would not have the same kind of control if taxation originated in the Senate, where representatives have six years between elections instead of two.

Harry Reid violated this clause when he introduced Obamacare. The Affordable Care Act was defined by the Supreme Court as a tax bill, but it appears to have originated in the Senate. If only our leaders had followed the letter of the Constitution, we might have been spared the frustrations of this ill-advised legislation.

Fortunately, the Constitution provides checks and balances to Congress's power of legislation in case of such abuses. For a bill to be passed by either house of Congress, a simple majority of affirmative votes is needed. A bill that is passed by both houses of Congress becomes law only after it has been reviewed and accepted by the president. This provision of our Constitution dramatically demonstrates the enormous power vested in the office of the president of the United States. With a stroke of the pen, the president can affirm or derail the efforts of hundreds of legislators who represent the will of the people. If that will is strong enough, though, Congress can override a presidential veto with a two-thirds majority in both houses.

The veto provision exists to preclude the hasty passage of unwise laws, and our founders did not anticipate that its use would be necessary often.[2] But today if a president has an agenda that to him is more important than the will of the people, he is likely to use the veto pen (or at least threaten to use it) on a regular basis. This should serve as a warning to the people that they must carefully watch the actions of such a president and his supporters in Congress. They must be willing to vote out of office all such people who have agendas that are not consistent with the will of the people.

This system of checks and balances works well when the president and the legislators love their country and have its best interests at heart. It works less well when a majority of the officials are more concerned about their own power or that of their political party than they are about the general welfare of the nation. A wise and vigilant electorate will be able to discern which of their representatives are simply political hacks and which ones are truly concerned about the welfare of all of the people.

TAXES

Having learned their lesson from inability of the federal government to raise funds under the Articles of Confederation, the founders wrote into the Constitution the ability for Congress to impose enough taxes to meet the financial needs of the government. If the size and scope of the government are reasonable and the taxation system is fair and unbiased, the system should work quite well. On the other hand, if the size and scope of the government and its programs are too great, taxation becomes burdensome and necessarily unfair.

In section 8 of Article 1 the founders outlined the rules for direct and indirect taxation and mandated that taxation be spread evenly across the country. A constitutional amendment, as well as multiple court cases, have adjusted the guidelines for taxation since then, but the main principles remain constant: The founders wanted to be sure the government could fund itself, to prevent the redistribution of wealth from one part of the country to another and to limit tyrannical taxation. Their foresight in recognizing these potential problems is truly a blessing for which we should be quite grateful.

CONGRESS'S SPECIFIC POWERS

Much of the Constitution is devoted to stating what the federal government *cannot* do. In section 8 of Article 1, we see instead a list of Congress's positive powers. From borrowing money to regulating trade to establishing an army, Congress has the right to do whatever is "necessary and proper" to keep the country moving.

Borrowing

The founders recognized that there might arise situations when the government would need large amounts of cash beyond what was available through the United States Treasury. Accordingly, they gave Congress the power to take out loans. However, our early leaders were also concerned about leaving debt to the next generation and expended great energy to remain fiscally solvent.

Trade

The Constitution gives Congress complete control over all trade between the United States and foreign countries. Congress is in charge of making sure that we don't export products that are badly needed in this country and that we don't bring in from other countries things that would be harmful to this nation. Congress also protects American businesses and industries from unfair foreign competition through the use of tariffs and taxes and other legal maneuvers.

Interstate commerce also comes under congressional authority. Interstate roadways, railroads, air travel, and electronic communications are all regulated by the federal government. It doesn't take a great deal of imagination to see that attempting to regulate these things on a state-by-state basis, with each state having a different agenda, would create an untenable situation.

For similar reasons no state is allowed to enter into a trade agreement with another nation. Domestic commerce also is controlled on the national level, which prevents the states from taxing one another in an unfair manner. This is all part of promoting domestic tranquillity.

Immigration and Citizenship

When it comes to immigration, Congress alone has the power to decide who can become an American citizen. No foreigner has a right to American citizenship, even if he or she has managed to evade authorities and slip into the country illegally. The rules that are created by our congressional representatives regarding immigration, both legal and illegal, should conform to the will of the American people. At no point should Congress or the executive branch unilaterally decide to pass immigration policy that is opposed by the majority of American citizens who have worked hard to build a desirable nation.

Fortunately, the United States remains a dream destination for people all over the world. This means we can formulate laws that allow us to pick the cream of the crop based on our needs as a country. If we are wise, we can significantly strengthen our country by creating and enforcing immigration policies that bring talent and resources to our country. If we are unwise, our policies will bring in people who must be supported rather than those who contribute.

Bankruptcy Law

Many of our founders saw while living in other countries the devastating effect that bankruptcy could have on an individual and his or her family. By giving Congress the power to pass laws to protect individuals who owe money as well as those to whom it is owed, they afforded protection from extreme abuse on a fair basis. Congress should seldom bail people or institutions out of financial trouble when they have brought it upon themselves through poor business decisions, but at the same time Congress has to evaluate the overall effect of large bankruptcies on the general welfare of the nation.

The recent bailouts of General Motors, Chrysler, AIG, and some other large financial players happened because our government decided that the bankruptcies of these entities would have such a negative impact on the entire nation that exceptions should be made. It is hard to know whether or not these were the right decisions, but I hope lessons were learned both by our government and by the private sector about risky financial dealings with other people's money. Many of the lessons that were learned after the stock-market crash in 1929 and in the ensuing years were forgotten as time went on. We have had two opportunities to learn important lessons about risky financial behavior, and I hope that will be enough.

Money

Congress has the power to design our money and to determine how much it is worth. This applies to both paper money and coins, which have to be uniform throughout the country. Initially our money was based on foreign coins and then precious metals, but more recently it has been based on our good name and credit. There are some countries in the world that are trying to return to a gold standard, and they could present a challenge to our system at some point in the future, particularly if we do not get our debt under control. We do have enough time to take care of this problem if we don't play ostrich and stick our heads in the sand.

Congress also has the power to establish a single system of weights and measures, which is important to the unity of the nation. Obviously, the use of different measurements in different parts of the country would create enormous difficulty and problems with commerce. Similarly, counterfeiting money is a federal offense because it has the potential to create havoc in our financial markets. For this reason congressional oversight of this offense is warranted.

The Post Office

Congress is given the authority to establish a postal system, which of course benefits the expansion and development of the nation. This includes authority to develop the various routes for mail delivery, including land, sea, and air. Congress also ensures that we have standardized postal rates and a dependable national distribution system at a reasonable price.

Copyright Law

Congress also has power "to promote the Progress of Science and useful Arts, by securing for limited Times to Authors and Inventors the exclusive Right to their respective Writings and Discoveries." This clause is one of the things that made America into a great destination for creative people. It created an environment that was conducive to innovation and creativity, and our country was and has been richly rewarded with unimaginable talent that has brought wealth, advancement, and entertainment to millions.

Some have criticized our system, because they do not believe that individuals should be able to benefit financially from good ideas that are useful to everyone. They feel that everything should belong to everyone. This is one of the big differences between capitalism and communism. An objective comparison of the communist system and the capitalist system will quickly demonstrate that our system has far outperformed any communist system on the planet. Fortunately, we are also blessed with the most generous society in the world, and I hope we will always encourage people to share the wealth.

Lower Courts

The judicial branch of government includes not only the Supreme Court of the United States but also the federal court system as established by the Congress. The federal courts can be set up and changed as needed by the Congress. The courts of appeals, the district courts, the Court of Claims, and the tax court are among the courts that have been established for specific purposes by Congress. If for some reason this court system is not functioning properly, Congress has the ability to restructure or adjust it.

International Relations

Congress also has the power to enforce orderly conduct outside the boundaries of the United States when our citizens are involved. Through Congress, we have the ability to protect and control all of our ships as well as our citizens even when they are outside of our nation. When our citizens commit crimes or misdemeanors in other countries, they still have protective rights that can be worked out by cooperating with the nation involved. When the United States projects an image of great strength and consistency, the likelihood of people and governments in other parts of the world interfering with our citizens decreases significantly.

Only Congress has the legal authority to declare war. It will generally do so only when the interests of our nation are at stake, and that includes the lives of our citizens. This power is given to Congress because its members represent the people of the country and are likely to engage in a study of the facts before making a hasty decision about war. Sometimes the president, who is the commander in chief, has to quickly engage our armed forces in combat roles, which can be seen as a declaration of war. This happened after the attack on our forces in Pearl Harbor in 1941 and again in 2001 after the attacks on the Pentagon and the World Trade Center on 9/11. In these cases Congress met to declare that a state of war existed.

The provision about granting letters of marque and reprisal was important in the past, when private United States citizens actually commanded ships that were prepared for battle and sometimes were able to capture enemy vessels. Obviously this is no longer the case, but Congress still has the power to establish rules for capturing property of our enemies outside of this country. There have been times in the past when we have captured land and assets of our adversaries, and there may be future times when that will again become necessary. Assets also include enemy combatants, and their treatment should be under congressional control.

Congress has a great deal of military authority when it comes to establishing and supporting the needs of our armed forces. It can compel citizens to join the armed forces and it can compel them to adhere to military laws. Congress supplies the money to support our military endeavors, but the founders mandated that no more than two years of financial support could be provided at once, so that Congress would have continuous control over the military. If enough money were supplied to support ten years of military activities, the military might decide to ignore Congress and establish its own authority. Today the military is funded on an annual basis.

State Militias

The rule of law is important to the survival and advancement of any society. Our founders recognized that civil unrest with widespread rioting, looting, and violence would undermine the authority of the government and shake the confidence of the populace. This was the reason for the formation of state militias, which have morphed into the National Guard of today. Initially these were funded by the states, but now they are largely funded by the federal government. They consist of ordinary citizens who have been trained to use military tactics and weaponry to maintain order. They can be used in the same capacity as the regular military and in fact can be called to serve as active-duty participants when necessary. Even though they are called the National Guard, each unit remains under the control of the respective state governors.

Washington, DC

Congress has control over the District of Columbia, which is the seat of our national government. Washington, DC, has a mayor, a city council, and commissioners, but because it is the headquarters of our national government, it is truly governed by Congress. The federal government has historically purchased a great deal of property throughout the United States, such as national parks, post offices, and historical sites. This makes our government by far the largest landowner in the country. It is responsible for the maintenance of these vast properties. There is no requirement that the government own so many national resources, and this may be an appropriate topic for Congress to take up in the future.

"Necessary and Proper"

Finally, Congress has power "to make all Laws which shall be necessary and proper for carrying into Execution the foregoing Powers, and all other powers vested by this Constitution in the Government of the United States, or in any Department or Officer thereof." This part of the Constitution has been called the "elastic clause," because it gives Congress the ability to interpret virtually any law or rule in a way that will allow it to carry out its duties. The powers of Congress can be stretched in unimaginable ways through application of this clause, but fortunately there are 535 members of Congress, which means that there is little likelihood that the clause will be severely abused. If, however, Congress oversteps its boundaries, our system of checks and balances allows it to be reined in by the executive branch or the judicial branch.

LIMITS ON FEDERAL POWER

In keeping with the spirit of limited government, the Constitution includes restrictions on Congress's powers in section 9 of Article 1.

Slavery

In an unfortunate concession to representatives of slave states, the first clause in Article 1: section 9 states that Congress could not ban the importation of slaves, which would have been a tremendous economic detriment to Southern states. As a concession to the abolitionists, however, the clause allows for the imposition of such a ban after 1808. Though this clause is still in the Constitution, slavery was of course abolished by the Thirteenth Amendment in 1865.

Habeas Corpus

Most people have heard of the right of habeas corpus, mentioned in Article 1, but relatively few actually know what it means. The term is Latin and literally means "you have the body." Essentially it means that the government is not allowed to hold someone prisoner without bringing him or her before a judge in a timely fashion.

This is an important right, because in many other countries, the rulers can have people arrested and jailed for life without cause. Or they can issue trumped-up charges that never have to be justified. In our system the arrested person can insist that the jailer present the arrestee and the case to a judge within a reasonable amount of time. If the judge determines that the person should be held, the arrested one must be charged with a crime. If there is no criminal charge, the person must be set free. In the case of massive civil unrest or war, habeas corpus can be temporarily suspended but is reactivated immediately upon restoration of peace and calm.

Legitimate Trials

"No Bill of Attainder or ex post facto Law shall be passed." A bill of attainder is a decree by a legislature to punish someone without the benefit of a legitimate trial. This was a common practice in the Old World and our founders wanted no part of it in our nation. Obviously, if such a thing could be done, no one would dare disagree with the government. Through political correctness, many still try to silence disagreement, but fortunately we have not reached the stage where official punishment ensues.

"Ex post facto" is a Latin term that means "after the fact." The founders wanted to make sure that the government did not punish people for activities they had engaged in before such activities were declared illegal. Obviously, without this provision, it would be possible to pass a law to punish anyone you didn't agree with based on any action they had carried out. As ridiculous as this sounds, it was a common practice in the Old World and happens in some dictatorial regimes even today.

Limits on Taxes

"No Capitation, or other direct, Tax shall be laid, unless in Proportion to the Census or enumeration herein before directed to be taken." A capitation tax directly collects money from every citizen "per capita." According to this part of the Constitution, any such tax would have to be the same for the people of each state. Congress has rarely levied direct taxes upon the citizens of our nation, with the federal income tax (enacted in 1913) being a notable exception.

"No Tax or Duty shall be laid on Articles exported from any State." This clause allows manufacturers in the various states to trade with other countries without the imposition of onerous taxes by Congress. It encourages a friendly business atmosphere, which is one of the reasons why the United States of America rose to the economic pinnacle of the world in less than one hundred years after the Declaration of Independence.

"No Preference shall be given by any Regulation of Commerce or Revenue to the Ports of one State over those of another: nor shall Vessels bound to, or from, one State be obliged to enter, clear, or pay Duties in another." Under this clause Congress cannot play favorites among the various states. This is an important clause because some states are much bigger than others and have many times as many of representatives in the House of Representatives. Without this type of safeguard, those representatives might be tempted to craft legislation favoring their individual states. This clause also facilitates the state-to-state travel of commercial vessels.

"No Money shall be drawn from the Treasury, but in Consequence of Appropriations made by Law; and a regular Statement and Account of the Receipts and Expenditures of all public Money shall be published from time to time." This means that the only monies from the U.S. Treasury that can be spent by public officials are those designated by specific laws for specific spending. Meticulous records have to be kept so that every penny can be accounted for. The records of all such spending must be available to the public.

Limits on "Royalty"

Most of our founders were less than amused by the whole concept of royalty and were determined to obliterate any trace of such a thing from American soil. They declared that no titles of nobility should be granted by the country and that no American ruler should accept such titles from other countries. The whole concept of royalty is antithetical to the American way of life. We sometimes treat our athletes and movie stars as if they were royalty, when in fact they are no different from anyone else. We must always cling vigorously to the concept of equality under the law.

LIMITS ON STATE POWER

The Constitution makes it clear that the states retain all powers not specifically given to the government, but the founders wisely spelled out a few limitations. Clearly, if the states were able to do such things as make alliances with other countries, coin money, or enact laws that conflicted with federal laws, a state of anarchy would soon exist. Accordingly, in section 10 of Article 1, the Constitution declares the limits on state power. States may not arbitrarily punish people without a legal trial. They may not institute export or import taxes. No state is to maintain an army, go to war, or set up a treaty on its own.

LAWS FOR LIBERTY

Article 1 is by far the most extensive and detailed part of the Constitution. Recognizing that the power to write laws is the power to control lives, the founders were careful to examine every detail of legislative power. Because of their care, we are free from tyrants today, but this freedom isn't guaranteed. It is our responsibility to responsibly consider amendments that may be required by modern developments. Even more important, it is our responsibility to see that the existing restrictions are upheld. If we are faithful to these responsibilities, our legislative branch will continue to represent the American people, and we will preserve "liberty and justice for all."

CHAPTER 10
ARTICLE 2, THE EXECUTIVE BRANCH

"A king detests wrongdoing, for his rule is built on justice."

Proverbs 16:12

Early in 2012 President Obama appointed a new director of the Consumer Financial Protection Bureau without congressional consent. He felt that his appointments were being politicized, and he was growing increasingly impatient with what he perceived as unfair treatment by the legislative branch of government, so he flouted constitutional standards. A president can get away with this kind of cowboylike activity if Congress backs down and simply complains without taking action. My hope is that citizens will learn what the Constitution says about the executive branch and will elect congresspeople who will uphold its standards.

The president shouldn't need others to force him to uphold the Constitution. When presidents take office, they swear the oath written in section 1 of Article 2 of the Constitution: "I do solemnly swear (or affirm) that I will faithfully execute the Office of President of the United States, and will to the best of my Ability, preserve, protect and defend the Constitution of the United States."

When a new president is inaugurated, the new leader is stepping into the most powerful position in the United States of America. Recognizing this, the founders took the role seriously and devoted Article 2 to defining the powers and procedures of the position. The article sets in place definite limits on executive authority, and the founders made it clear that their intent was to err on the side of lessening executive power.

Congress limits the president's power to executing the laws passed by Congress. The president may not legislate and is given power only to make sure that the will of the people, as expressed through Congress, is carried out. Anything else is overreach.

The founders had personally experienced the horrors of living under tyrannical rulers who were interested only in their own personal gain and felt no compassion for the people. They were especially concerned about potential overreaches by the executive branch of government, because it was led by a single individual, the president, who could become intoxicated with power and establish a de facto monarchy. The executive branch also controls the military, increasing the danger if any president were to become a dictator.

To prevent executive abuse, the framers enabled Congress and the courts to rein in executive overreach. Congress can defund virtually any governmental department or program and every presidential perk. The courts can declare an executive action illegal. By having three separate but equal branches of government, each of which would be interested in maintaining its power and influence, the founders believed that a representative government could be achieved on a long-term basis.

These days Congress is divided. This provides a distinct advantage for the executive branch if it truly wants to engage in power grabbing. Congress must once again concentrate on becoming an effective body, and not just to prevent presidential power grabs. It is my hope that readers of this chapter will recapture the founders' original vision for the presidency and will elect presidents who fit that vision and congresspeople who will uphold all of the details of the second article of the Constitution.

THE PRESIDENT'S POSITION AND HIS STAFF

Article 2 begins by defining the executive branch, which today includes the office of the president, the office of the vice president, all of the cabinet departments, and the president's administrative staff. The president has a staff of thousands to help with his numerous executive duties. No one person can effectively deal with the thousands of issues that arise on a daily basis, so the president is wise to depend on capable individuals with expertise in a variety of different areas. Failure to do so will almost certainly result in a failed presidency.

The office of the vice president is less well defined, and the vice president in many ways is a utility player, filling in where needed. A vice president with particular expertise in a problem area can be a tremendous asset to the president and to the country. Aside from that, he or she must be fully competent to assume the duties of the president in case of the president's death or incapacitation. And, of course, the vice president acts as the president of the Senate.

PRESIDENTIAL ELECTIONS

Though most Americans are more aware of presidential elections than of any other election, few really understand how the electoral process works, assuming that the voters elect the president directly. But that's not how the founders set things up. In fact, between the modified electoral college and party politics, our presidential elections bear little resemblance to the system described in Article 2.

Rather than having the general public elect the president, the writers of our Constitution wanted an engaged group of people who were knowledgeable about political events to choose executive officials. Accordingly, section 1 of Article 2 states that the state legislatures should choose "electors." The number of electors designated for each state was to be determined by the combined number of senators and representatives that each state had in Congress. There was no mechanism for all of these electors to meet together, so each state's electors were to vote in the state's capital. Each state's electoral votes were to be reported to the president of the U.S. Senate, who would tally the votes and present the results publicly.

In the original plan the Electoral College votes were to be counted in Congress. The person receiving the most votes would become president, and the one receiving the second-most votes would become vice president. This resulted in bizarre teams—imagine if Al Gore had become George W. Bush's vice president because he came in second. Having a president and vice president of different political persuasions meant the executive branch was far from united. Even worse, the setup incentivized assassination, because the death of a president could benefit the other party. After one of these pairings (Democratic-Republican Thomas Jefferson serving under Federalist John Adams), Congress decided a change was needed. In 1804 the Twelfth Amendment changed the electoral process to solve this problem. The Twelfth Amendment requires electors to indicate both the person they want for president and the person they want for vice president.

The system of electors is still in place. This means that when you vote for president, you are really voting for an elector who you think will vote for the candidate you prefer. In reality, electors do not have to vote for the candidate they are associated with, but it is rare for an elector to renege on the expectation.

If the American populace becomes more involved with the political process and the number of voters increases, it might be worthwhile to move to a popular-vote model. In the meantime, we must work with the system we have, electoral college and all.

POLITICAL PARTIES

We also have to reckon with the reality of political parties, even though the two-party system was not in existence when the Constitution was written. Today the candidates for president and vice president are chosen by the parties. This began with the first national political party convention in 1827. At first, these conventions highlighted many candidates and the politics of its particular party. Party leaders from throughout the country held national conventions to nominate a presidential and vice presidential candidate. Since the 1970s, now before the conventions the party's candidates compete against one another for votes and are assigned delegates based on how well they do in state primary elections. Those delegates attend party conventions and vote for their candidates. The first candidate to reach the requisite number of delegate votes generally wins the nomination as the party's candidate to run for president. That individual then has the opportunity to choose as his or her running mate any eligible citizen of the United States.

Another important function of the political conventions is the establishment of the party platform. Each party formulates a statement of its beliefs and values and goals. It is important for voters to read these platforms and be familiar with them. Many people would be surprised if they actually familiarized themselves with the platform of the party that traditionally garners their support.

Under the party system, politics becomes at least as important as substance. The unity of our nation should trump any political considerations, but politicians often end up being loyal to their party at the expense of the nation. Politicians become so involved in making the other party look bad that they are unable to recognize the destructive tendencies of their partisan philosophical bickering. When issues like demanding transparent inspections of Iranian nuclear facilities become political issues, we are in trouble. Our leaders should be able to unite around existential threats instead of trying to score a point off the opposing party.

Because of the toxicity of the two-party system, many outstanding citizens will not even consider entering the political arena. The environment has changed so dramatically from the days of the founders that ordinary citizens are out of place in Washington, and professional politicians rule the day. This is not the vision of Article 2, and it's time "we the people" rise above the political infighting and choose sensible executives based on their qualifications, not the letters after their names.

THE PRESIDENT'S QUALIFICATIONS, SUCCESSORS, AND SALARY

Because of the level of wisdom needed to successfully occupy the office of president of the United States of America, the age and experience qualifications for the job are stricter than those for other positions in the federal government. The Constitution requires that the president be a natural-born citizen, be at least thirty-five years old, and have been a resident of the United States for at least fourteen years.

The presidency is an extremely stressful job that requires the ability to multitask and remain calm in the face of disaster. Thus it makes sense to elect a person of maturity. The president also must have no divided loyalties—thus the citizenship requirement. Though many immigrants have strong loyalty to America, it would be an unmitigated disaster to elect someone president who was not a natural-born citizen and who did not really have the best interests of the United States at heart. And, of course, the White House occupant should have lived in the United States long enough to be familiar with its culture and values.

In the event of the death or disability of the president, the vice president steps into the office, followed by the Speaker of the House and the president pro tempore of the Senate. Until 1947, the Constitution mandated that the vice president be followed by the secretary of state and then various other cabinet members. An amendment changed that in order to better honor the will of the people. Cabinet members are not elected officials and therefore should not be the first people to take the helm of the country if a disaster removes both the president and the vice president.

In keeping with the goal of honoring the will of the people, the Constitution states that the president's salary cannot be changed during his term. If Congress could adjust the president's salary, the legislative branch would have too much power over the executive branch, because politicians could manipulate the president's salary as a bribe or punishment.

PRESIDENTIAL POWERS

Once in office, the president has an impressive array of powers, from controlling the military to entering into treaties. A strong president will make the most of these powers—and a wise president will know how to use them to serve the people and keep the peace. During the civil rights struggle of the sixties, the president was able to move military forces into the areas of conflict to prevent bloodshed. The same was true during the Detroit riots in 1967 and multiple other civil disturbances throughout the United States over the years.

As the commander in chief of the military, the president has the power to move equipment and command military forces. The president is not a member of the military, because civilian rule of the military is very important to freedom. Instead, the president is to lead and respect the troops as a civilian leader. No president has the power to start a war without the approval of Congress, though the Constitution does give the president the power to respond quickly to threats and to temporarily declare martial law and suspend rights like freedom of the press and habeas corpus if there is an urgent threat. For instance, both Franklin Delano Roosevelt and Harry Truman were able to make quick decisions during World War II that made a huge difference. If President Roosevelt had been forced to wait for Congress to pass measures allowing the United States to honor Winston Churchill's request for aid, the war might have ended badly. If President Truman had been required to seek congressional approval for deployment of the Tuskegee airmen or for the use of atomic weapons, an endless debate might have ensued and the entire civil rights movement and the end of the war might have been delayed. The founders were wise to allow the executive branch to efficiently exercise this kind of power in emergencies. Fortunately, the times when this has been required have been rare.

Another power of the president is the power of pardon, which allows the president to waive sentences when people are wrongly convicted or when there are mitigating circumstances. The president is forbidden to grant pardons only in cases of impeachment, as that might involve a conflict of interest and would negate the legislative branch's power of impeachment. When used wisely, the power to pardon serves mercy and justice. However, voters should carefully track pardons granted by the president, because the power can be abused.

The Constitution also grants the president the power to make treaties and other agreements with foreign powers. Although the president approves and gets credit for these treaties, legions of hardworking public servants laboring under the direction of the secretary of state actually hammer out the agreements. Because the treaties often have significant implications for the economy or safety of the United

States, they must be approved by two thirds of the Senate before they are activated. There are a host of foreign agreements that do not reach the level of importance of an international treaty, and these can be activated with only the signature of the president and do not require congressional approval.

The president is also allowed to nominate individuals to occupy important governmental positions. For example, the president appoints Supreme Court justices, federal judges, cabinet officers, the federal communications commissioner, high military officials, and the directors of the National Institutes of Health, Federal Reserve Board, Interstate Commerce Commission, and Atomic Energy Commission.

Of course, the president does not personally know all of the best candidates for these kinds of positions. To make sure good candidates are chosen, teams of researchers evaluate candidates and then make recommendations to the president. Due to their importance, all of these positions must be approved by a majority vote in the Senate. If a critical position requiring congressional approval becomes vacant while Congress is in recess, the president is permitted to make an interim appointment to fill the position until such time as Congress is able to reassemble and approve or reject the appointment.

Appointments don't always go unopposed. In the early 1990s President George H. W. Bush nominated Judge Clarence Thomas to be an associate justice of the Supreme Court. Many members of Congress were opposed to the nomination because Thomas was a conservative and was black. Many members of the progressive political class have difficulty accepting the concept of a black conservative. People who are truly objective and fair realize that anyone has a right to formulate his or her political ideas regardless of racial identity. I hope that at some point in the near future, we as a nation can get beyond this foolishness. After what the *Washington Post* called one of the most contentious and public confirmation hearings in American history,[1] Thomas was confirmed, but many deep wounds were opened, with implications lasting even until today.

The Constitution also refers to inferior officers who can be appointed by the president or his designees without congressional approval. Congress has vested in the president the power to put in place people with whom he or she feels comfortable working in order to accomplish important goals and objectives. Many of these appointees will also hire their own staffs, who will also technically be considered part of the executive branch.

The vast majority of these government jobs are "civil service" jobs and are available to any American citizen capable of passing the requisite examination for the job. Usually those with the highest scores are awarded the jobs. This is a vast improvement over the old "spoils systems," in which government jobs were rewards for political supporters.

Unfortunately, the number of civil-service jobs, in both the executive and the legislative and judicial branches, has grown out of control. The federal budget represents a significant portion of the gross domestic product, partly because of oversized staffs and partly because of redundancy and waste. Some years ago I was involved as an expert witness in a government case, and I was told that I could charge whatever amount of money I wanted to charge. I have encountered others with similar accounts of what they were told, and it was quite distressing to me to realize that people were playing fast and loose with hard-earned taxpayer dollars. This is not a Democratic or Republican problem; rather it is an American problem that needs to be addressed soon, before we further compromise the future of our nation.

Some will argue that the livelihoods of so many Americans depend on government jobs that it would be cruel to cut back on government positions. It is true that many of these jobholders have done nothing wrong, and we must use compassion in dealing with their careers. That said, a change must happen. The logical solution is to reduce government size by attrition. Thousands of government employees retire every year, and we would be wise not to replace them. Critical positions that are vacated could be filled by shifting people from other positions in the government who had the requisite skills. If this were done for a few years, substantial reductions in government payroll could be accomplished without firing innocent people. The president would still have powers of appointment, but the number of unnecessary positions would be reduced.

With all of the powers of the office, the president of the United States is the most powerful person in the world. Bearing in mind the danger of being corrupted by such power, a wise president will organize a carefully selected group of advisers, called the cabinet, referred to in section 2 of Article 2 as the group of "the principal Officer[s] of each of the executive Departments." Currently the cabinet consists of the secretary of state, secretary of the treasury, secretary of defense, attorney general, secretary of the interior, secretary of agriculture, secretary of commerce, secretary of labor, secretary of health and human services, secretary of housing and urban development, secretary of transportation, secretary of energy, secretary of education, secretary of veterans affairs, and secretary of homeland security. There are also several other cabinet-level positions, including White House chief of staff, director of the Office of Management and Budget, administrator of the Environmental Protection Agency, trade representative, ambassador to the United Nations, chairman of the Council of Economic Advisers, and administrator of the Small Business Administration.

The book of Proverbs states that "in the multitude of counselors is safety," and the founders were wise to suggest a group of advisers. Power wielded alone is dangerous, and a wise chief executive will listen to people who agree with him, as well as those who have other opinions, in order to make the wisest possible choice.

PRESIDENTIAL RESPONSIBILITY AND ACCOUNTABILITY

Under section 3 of Article 2, the president is responsible for communicating to the nation, making sure that crises are addressed, and seeing that the law of the land is executed. The president has quite a bit of leeway in how these duties are carried out, but the duties are not optional.

Each year the president reports to Congress on the "State of the Union" and suggests policy measures that he thinks might improve the nation's welfare. This annual address is important for more than political reasons. The president acts as the end of a funnel of information gathered from the hundreds of thousands of federal employees throughout the world. These employees are involved in national defense, business and industry, finance, education, social services, science, and a host of other fields. The State of the Union address gives the president the opportunity to impart to Congress the important information he has gleaned, along with suggestions for the advancement of the country.

The president also has the ability to call special sessions of Congress in order to accomplish important business of the nation. For instance, special sessions were called by President Madison during the War of 1812, by President Lincoln to deal with the secession of the Southern states, and by President Roosevelt to reveal the first hundred days of the New Deal.

Section 3 of Article 2 of the Constitution specifically states that the president "shall take Care that the Laws be faithfully executed." Notice that it does not say that he should take care that the laws with which he agrees be faithfully executed. The president and the rest of the executive branch cannot pick and choose the laws they wish to enforce while ignoring others. To do so is to renege upon their responsibilities to uphold the Constitution of the United States of America.

If the president doesn't carry out the required tasks faithfully, he or she can be impeached. If the president or any other members of the executive branch are found guilty of engaging in activities that are counterproductive to the well-being of America, they should be quickly removed from office before they inflict more damage. America's leaders should be examples of integrity and high moral standards. When their behavior evokes shame rather than pride and becomes something that we don't want to discuss in front of the children at the kitchen table, we should consider impeachment.

The founders of our nation understood that decency was a large part of good government. John Adams went so far as to state that "our Constitution was made only for a moral and religious people. It is wholly inadequate to the government of any other."[2] What he was really saying is that we can maintain our freedom only when a certain degree of common decency and respect for one's fellow man is present. If we have no values and principles upon which we can generally agree, it becomes every man for himself, and unity becomes a distant dream. Certainly the president should be the foremost example of that kind of integrity.

THE PRESIDENCY TODAY

Today our nation is in such shambles that it appears that almost anyone could do a better job of execution than the current leaders. The principal problem appears to be a lack of congruency between the president and the people. His goal seems to be a utopian society managed by the government, rather than the free, self-governing society that the founders left us. Americans want to be free, and the president's approval ratings indicate that "we the People" do not agree with his goals. I pray that the next president will have a set of values that matches those of the majority of Americans. I pray that he will use his power to encourage the "can-do" attitude that characterized America's rapid ascent to the pinnacle of the world.

CHAPTER 11
ARTICLE 3, THE JUDICIAL BRANCH

"The Lord demands accurate scales and balances;
he sets the standards for fairness."

Proverbs 16:11

From 1983 to 1984 I was the senior registrar in neurosurgery at the Sir Charles Gairdner Hospital of the Queen Elizabeth II Medical Centre in Perth, Western Australia. One evening that year my wife and I were driving down a long hill. At the base of that hill was a speed trap where the police ticketed just about everyone who picked up speed coming down the hill.

To say that the car we were driving was not capable of speeding would be a drastic understatement. It was a very economical four-cylinder model that was little more than a skateboard with a motor. Nevertheless, an officer stopped us and issued a speeding citation. I protested, stating that my car was not capable of the speed he accused us of, but to no avail. The officer suggested that I meet him in court, which I did.

I was quite sorry that I had gone to court when I witnessed how brutal the judge was. Most of the defendants had lawyers, and I was there by myself, regretting my decision. When it came time for me to approach the bench and explain my situation, I informed the judge that the police had been using radar equipment that operated on the Doppler effect. This meant that the signal could be substantially degraded by angulation such as we encountered on the hill. After further explanations, the judge simply said, "Case dismissed." I felt vindicated and happy with the Australian judicial system that particular day.

When the American judicial system works well, the judges also listen to reason. As Article 3 makes clear, the duty of the judicial branch is to interpret the laws that are created by the legislative branch and enforced by the executive branch of government. Its job is to protect the people from overly aggressive executive and legislative branches of government that might from time to time forget that they are in fact the servants of the people rather than the rulers of the people.

The Supreme Court of the United States sits at the pinnacle of the federal judicial system and is responsible for the interpretation of laws. If Congress passes a law that violates the Constitution, the Supreme Court can strike it down. If there's a question as to how exactly a law applies to a particular situation, the Court rules on that too.

Congress has the right to establish other federal courts that are less powerful than the Supreme Court but still have important duties. Most legal cases are handled in these "inferior" courts, which are any courts whose decisions can be appealed to a higher court. That includes all state courts and all federal courts besides the U.S. Supreme Court.

In order to make sure that judicial officials are not easily intimidated, the Constitution protects their salaries and in many cases gives them lifetime appointments. Unfortunately, this shielding can damage as well as preserve America's freedoms. Some judges are so protected from the public's reactions to their judgments that they've lost sight of the will of the people. There have been several instances where voters through a ballot referendum chose one thing, only to have judges come along, decide that the voters had no idea what they were talking about, and overturn the will of the voters.

It is unlikely that it was the intention of the founders to give any public official the ability to thwart the will of the people. Although they may have been concerned about mob rule and wanted a judicial system that would prevent that, they also recognized that in many other countries it was assumed that the ruling class always knew better than the people, and they wanted no part of such a system.

Recognizing that judges might abuse their power, the founders included in the Constitution a phrase that would give Congress the ability to remove such judges. They said that judges "shall hold their Offices during good Behavior." There is some room for interpretation of what "good Behavior" means, but when one understands that the Constitution was established to protect the will of the people, it becomes clear that it is a serious offense to thwart that will. The vast majority of federal judges are outstanding American citizens who uphold the rights of the people, but courage is required to move against the few bad apples that contaminate the system by ignoring the will of the people.

JURISDICTION

Federal courts can hear cases concerning the constitutionality of any law; treaties; shipping laws; and federal laws. These courts also have jurisdiction in cases where the involved parties are ambassadors, consuls, public ministers, the U.S. government, state governments in conflict with each other, or a citizen of one state suing a citizen of another. Cases involving foreigners or events occurring in foreign lands but involving American citizens are also within the jurisdiction of federal courts.

The vast majority of federal cases are handled in district courts quite satisfactorily. The Supreme Court does have the right to review the decisions made in all of the inferior courts and to change those decisions if it feels that they were improperly rendered. A case that has been tried in the lower court can be appealed through the appellate system all the way to the Supreme Court, but the Supreme Court is incapable of handling all the cases that are appealed due to the sheer volume. The Supreme Court has the ability to select which cases it chooses to hear. Fortunately, the appellate courts just below the Supreme Court, called the United States Courts of Appeals, generally do an excellent job in resolving outstanding issues.

JURIES AND JUSTICE

Whenever a person is accused of a serious crime, our Constitution provides the right to a trial by a jury of his or her peers. During the trial the facts are presented to the jury, and both the prosecuting attorney and the defense attorney make arguments before the jury. In cases of lesser crimes or misdemeanors, the defendant is frequently offered a choice between a trial by judge and a trial by jury.

The jury system works well but is by no means perfect. In medical-malpractice trials, a large portion of the case involves trying to educate the jury on what are sometimes complex medical issues. Victory frequently goes to whoever can put on the best dog and pony show rather than whoever has the facts on their side. This is one of the reasons why medical cases are frequently not even sent to a court in other countries, which have different mechanisms to take care of people who sustain injuries during medical treatment. The National Trial Lawyers, a special-interest group, has made every attempt to thwart the establishment of these kinds of mechanisms in the United States. This is because lawyers benefit financially from the current system. Lawyers and courts are an important part of a fair judicial system, but we clearly need some tort reform and need to invest time and energy in finding more appropriate ways to solve common societal problems.

When a case does go to trial, the Constitution requires the trial to take place in the state and region where the grievance occurred. This makes the likelihood of obtaining a trial by one's peers, people who actually understand the circumstances, much greater. Once again we see the founders' commitment to fairness for all citizens.

CRIMES

One of the crimes the Constitution is very clear about is treason. Treason is a crime punishable by death in America, as well as in many other countries. Because it is such a severe crime, the writers of the Constitution clearly defined the term. They said that treason meant warring against the United States, siding with her enemies, or assisting her enemies. Our founders were very specific about this because they knew that accusations of treason would otherwise be employed to get rid of political enemies.

In the last year or two a number of American citizens have traveled overseas and joined Islamic terrorist groups. This clearly would meet the definition of treason. Unfortunately, the definition of who our enemies are seems to be changing in America. Recently a high-profile income-tax official referred to Republicans as enemies. Others on the far right frequently refer to some Democrats as communists, socialists, or enemies of America. It is important that we tone down the rhetoric and stop allowing ourselves to be manipulated to the point that we believe that our fellow American citizens are enemies or are guilty of treason.

Once someone is convicted of treason, the Constitution is also clear about parameters for the traitor's punishment. The death penalty is not required and is seldom employed in this country today. The government also may not punish the family of the traitor. In modern America it seems unimaginable to punish the innocent children or relatives of a criminal who has committed treason against the United States. Nevertheless there is historical precedent for such actions in our mother country, Great Britain. The founders added this clause to ensure that we would never repeat the same kind of mistake in our country.

We should be grateful today that we live in a country where justice is valued. We should celebrate the good judges and juries that protect our liberty. We should make sure that our judges remember that their job is to judge, not to legislate or execute. And, though we should punish treason severely, we should remember that disagreement is not treason. As long as we stick to the principles outlined in Article 3, we will be able to maintain justice in our great nation.

CHAPTER 12
ARTICLES 4–7

"Remind everyone about these things, and command
them in God's presence to stop fighting over words. Such
arguments are useless, and they can ruin those who hear
them. Work hard so you can present yourself to God and
receive his approval. Be a good worker, one who does not
need to be ashamed and who correctly explains the word
of truth."

Timothy 2:14-15

I remember once being thrilled with a brand-new car I had purchased. The vehicle came with many fancy options that kept me occupied. Once I'd played with almost every gadget in the car, I decided to program the garage door opener. To my great dismay, it did not work. I had programmed many garage door openers over the years and felt quite competent in this area, but nothing I did worked. I finally gave up and decided to read the instruction manual, since all else had failed. It took only a minute of reading for me to learn that this door opener required a different method of programming than I had used before. I quickly adopted the new code and solved the problem. If only I had read the manual earlier, I would have saved myself a lot of frustration.

Similarly, many of the problems that we have in our nation could be solved by a careful reading of each of the articles of our Constitution. We may be convinced that we know everything there is to know about our Constitution, but speaking from my own experience, I learn something new almost every time I read it.

The last four articles of the Constitution are brief, but they deal with crucial points. Article 4 deals with the relationship between the states and the federal government. Article 5 outlines the steps to amend the Constitution. Article 6 makes it clear that the Constitution is the law of the land. Article 7 sets in place the steps for ratification.

ARTICLE 4: STATE AND FEDERAL GOVERNMENT

Article 4 of the Constitution deals with the relationship between the states and the federal government. Each state is to honor all legal actions taken in the other states. Without such a provision, we would be not one nation but fifty. With this provision every American citizen can move freely throughout the fifty states. If jobs are scarce in one state and plentiful in another, an American citizen can simply pull up roots and move to the location where jobs are plentiful. Because the language and culture are relatively uniform throughout the United States, this gives every citizen tremendous flexibility and choice.

You cannot vote in a state election unless you are a resident of that state. Fortunately, becoming a resident is a quick and simple process. All that is necessary is to establish a mailing address that is not a post office box and be able to prove that you actually live in the state. The amount of time that you are required to live in the state before applying for residency varies.

If the public records from one state were not available to the other states, mass confusion around identities and rights would prevail. If states didn't recognize marriages from other states, there would be chaos. If they didn't recognize the judgments of other state courts, people could simply move to a different state to avoid penalties for or consequences of their actions. As it is, the extradition requirement in Article 4 ensures in most cases that a criminal captured in another state will be returned to the state in which the crime was committed. Sometimes criminals have committed unlawful acts in multiple states and the issue of which state they should be returned to becomes quite complex. Fortunately, the relationships among various law-enforcement entities in the various states are strong and cordial.

In one case the friendly relationships among the states helped an evil cause, but fortunately a constitutional amendment put an end to the problem. One clause in Article 4 refers to slaves who had escaped from their owners, requiring that a slave who escaped to a free state be returned to his owner in a slave state if he was found. Fortunately, the Thirteenth Amendment abolished slavery, making this clause meaningless.

Another clause in Article 4 is also no longer necessary, though it has not been abolished. When the Constitution was written, the United States was in expansion mode, and its ambitious leaders wanted to ensure that the expansion was not at the expense of existing states. Thus they required that new states be added only with the approval of the existing states. Their intentions were realized, and the nation grew rapidly while the integrity of each state remained strong.

Today we are not looking to expand our territory, so the clause is rarely invoked.

Article 4 also has a clause giving Congress the power to govern U.S. territories that have not yet become states. The Louisiana Purchase, for example, encompassed a huge amount of territory that needed to be under the jurisdiction of the government. Once the Louisiana Territory, the Northwest Territory, and other such land parcels were developed into states, they fell under normal congressional regulation. This clause also allows Congress to set aside national parks and care for them, as well as build bridges, dams, and other projects to improve the quality of life of all American citizens.

Finally, Article 4 says that every state must have a republican form of government and guarantees that the federal government will protect individual states when threatened. This is a comforting section of the Constitution, because it guarantees that no state in the union will turn into a dictatorship. All Americans are guaranteed, both federally and at the state level, a form of government where the people select representatives who make the laws and where a constitution limits the power of government and protects the people. And when necessary, the federal government will step in to enforce this, as well as to protect the state from rioting, anarchy, or foreign invaders.

ARTICLE 5: AMENDING THE CONSTITUTION

In the 227 years since the Constitution of the United States was ratified, there have only been twenty-seven amendments to this amazing document. Many more than that have been proposed, but the framers of the Constitution wisely made the amendment process, outlined in Article 5, rather difficult, recognizing that there would always be those who are dissatisfied with the status quo and want change.

The framers were intelligent and well-read men who worked diligently for months on the document. Their strong desire was to create a constitution that would never allow the United States government to subvert the will of the people. But in their wisdom, the founders recognized that they were mortal creatures who could not know the future. They studied history and planned for the future, but they knew that a rapidly growing and changing nation would encounter situations they had not foreseen. The Constitution might need to be updated to address new circumstances, so the founders set in place procedures for amendment.

Any amendment to the Constitution must be presented to and approved by three quarters of the states. There are two ways an amendment can be proposed. First, two thirds of the states can petition Congress to call for a national convention, and the delegates to the convention can propose an amendment. Alternatively, if both houses of Congress agree, they can propose an amendment. This second option is far less cumbersome and, in fact, the first option has yet to be used. It usually makes more sense for states to propose an amendment through their already-elected national representatives than to go through the expense and complexity of a national convention.

Once an amendment has been proposed, it must be ratified in order to take effect. There are two methods of ratification, and Congress gets to decide which method will be used. The first method is for the state legislatures to approve the amendment. The second is for special conventions called by the states to approve the amendment. Regardless of which method is used, three quarters of the states must ratify the amendment to make it a part of the Constitution.

It really is quite amazing that our Constitution allows the people through their representatives to change the government. Historically, significant governmental changes have usually occurred through violence and revolution. This peaceful and orderly change process is truly exceptional and is one of the reasons why the United States has thrived.

Not everyone is content with peaceful change. Radical groups like the Weathermen, the Committees of Correspondence for Democracy and Socialism (CCDS), and the Party for Socialism and Liberation (PSL) have advocated deceit and violence as techniques for effecting governmental change. We should always be wary of those who want to fundamentally change our society without using the legitimate tools in place to do so.

Finally, Article 5 clearly indicates that the right of every state, no matter how small, to have two senators cannot be amended. This was one of the provisions that saved the union when there was so much disagreement about how the states would be represented, and it remains as a guarantee that the founders' compromise was not in vain.

ARTICLE 6: SOVEREIGNTY OF THE CONSTITUTION

The main purpose of Article 6 is to state unequivocally that the Constitution is the law of the land. The delegates knew they would need to make it clear to both the states and foreign powers that the Constitution overrode any earlier laws. They also needed to show that the new government under the Constitution was united and was prepared to look out for the interests of all of the states.

Accordingly, they declared in the first clause that all debts contracted by the United States before the adoption of the Constitution would still be recognized by the new government. This demonstrates the integrity of our government at the time of the writing of our Constitution. Historically when there was a change of regime, often those in charge of the new regime refused to pay back debts that the previous regime had incurred. Our fledgling nation refused to take the low road, and our first secretary of the treasury, Alexander Hamilton, agreed to pay back the estimated $77 million we owed, even though the bonds for this debt did not nearly cover the cost.[1] This is one of the reasons why even as a fledgling nation, the United States had an extremely good credit rating throughout the world. This began a long tradition of fiscal responsibility, which unfortunately disappeared several decades ago.

Article 6 also establishes the hierarchy of legislation in our nation. Laws made by the United States Congress are sovereign, those created by state legislatures are in the next tier, and local laws are subservient to those. In other words, a town legislature cannot make a law that contradicts the law of its state, and a state cannot make a law that contradicts a law made by Congress. One can only imagine the chaos that would ensue without this clause of the Constitution.

All government officials, whether federal, state, or local, are sworn to uphold the U.S. Constitution. We must all recognize that the many rights and freedoms we enjoy could evaporate rapidly if we do not jealously guard every aspect of this document. It has withstood the test of time and is partly responsible for the incredible accomplishments of this nation.

Although there is no specific mention of the separation of church and state in the Constitution, a clause in this article makes it clear that government positions should not be denied to anyone because of their religious affiliation, nor should any particular religious litmus test be applied to those seeking government employment. Our founders in many cases were men of great faith. Many of them had seen the societal harm that occurs when religion is suppressed or when it is elevated to a position of political control. They wanted to ensure that neither of these situations ever occurred in our nation. We should always be the beacon of religious freedom and tolerance, including the religion of atheism. We must always remember the concept of "live and let live," because it is one of the founding principles of our nation.

As long as we are the United States of America, the Constitution will be the supreme law, and we must do everything we can to make sure we uphold it. I pray that we will remember the principles of fiscal responsibility and religious freedom articulated in Article 6—we cannot remain free without them.

ARTICLE 7: RATIFICATION

The final article of the Constitution states that ratification by nine states would be sufficient for the Constitution to become the law of the land. The first state to ratify the Constitution was Delaware, followed by Pennsylvania, New Jersey, Georgia, Connecticut, Massachusetts, Maryland, South Carolina, New Hampshire, Virginia, and New York. After George Washington became president, North Carolina and Rhode Island also ratified the Constitution.[2]

The names of George Washington and the other thirty-nine signers ended the document.[3] These men placed their names on a document that would steer our country well for more than two hundred years—and counting. They were not perfect, and neither was the document they signed, but it recognized its own weaknesses and set in place countermeasures. You cannot ask for much more in this life.

CONCLUSION

As Articles 4 through 7 demonstrate, the founders thought they had done a pretty good job designing "a more perfect Union," so they made it difficult to undo their efforts. Fortunately, they were also humble enough to recognize that mechanisms for change would be needed. We can be thankful for that today; it is likely that those mechanisms will be needed in the not-too-distant future to establish term limits, something not needed in our nation's early days but desperately needed now.

We can feel confident that our Constitution is flexible enough to accommodate any necessary changes yet rigid enough to withstand unwarranted tampering. We are indeed fortunate to have had founders who were not only brilliant but also compassionate and wise. If we exercise those same characteristics going forward, the future for our children will be secured.

CHAPTER 13
THE BILL OF RIGHTS

"For the Lord is our judge, our lawgiver, and our king.
He will care for us and save us."

Isaiah 33:22

It wasn't long before Americans found the need to improve on the Constitution and passed the first ten amendments, known as the Bill of Rights. These were adopted in 1791, and many of them are much more familiar to the general public than is the Constitution itself. This is because the Bill of Rights specifically guarantees individual rights of citizens and is responsible for many of our freedoms today.

FIRST AMENDMENT

Congress shall make no law respecting an establishment of religion, or prohibiting the free exercise thereof; or abridging the freedom of speech, or of the press; or the right of the people peaceably to assemble, and to petition the Government for a redress of grievances.

Our Constitution was not designed to create uniformity of speech, behavior, or beliefs. Instead it was designed to ensure that everyone could live, speak, and believe as they pleased, as long as their actions did not infringe upon the rights of others. These incredibly important rights were not addressed in the Constitution, yet it is hard to imagine a United States without these safeguards.

Many of the founders of this nation and their ancestors had suffered religious persecution overseas and were acutely aware of the dangers of having a state-sponsored religion. A theocracy was clearly not the goal of the establishment of our nation, and this amendment guaranteed that we would never allow religion to dictate to government.

Looking back at the extreme intolerance manifested in the past by many religious groups, including some Christian groups, and looking today at the extreme intolerance of some radical Islamic groups, it is not hard to understand why our founders were so frightened of religion controlling government. The wall of separation between church and state is important and should be maintained. However, it should not be extended and reinterpreted as the separation of God and state.

There is nothing in our Constitution or its amendments to indicate that all vestiges of faith must be removed from the public square. This inappropriate extension of the concept of separation between church and state is in fact in direct opposition to the portion of the First Amendment that says Congress can make no law "prohibiting the free exercise thereof." This phrase means that no one should be prohibited from living a life of faith according to the dictates of conscience, as long as they are not harming others.

It becomes somewhat absurd when some claim that the sight of a Bible or a cross causes them so much psychological distress that it impinges upon their freedom. It is important that we learn to be reasonable and tolerant of everyone's beliefs without going to such extremes that we compromise everyone's rights.

The First Amendment also protects freedom of speech and freedom of the press. Suppression of freedom of speech is the ultimate manifestation of intolerance. Tyrants never want to be challenged, nor do they wish for others to hear anything that opposes their views. Dictators know that free speech may inspire suppressed populations to turn against them, so they quell speech through intimidation.

While we rarely see direct silencing of speech by the government in America today, there are other groups out to destroy free speech. On many college campuses in America today, conservative students and professors are intimidated into silence, and conservative speakers are not invited to give commencement addresses because the liberal administration does not wish for the students to be exposed to an alternative way of thinking.[1] This also occurs on some conservative campuses in the opposite direction, but to a much smaller degree. Rather than concentrate on assigning blame for this intolerance, we should concentrate on creating an open and stimulating environment for discussion, especially in our institutions of higher learning. After all, if our young people are not taught to value free speech, they may not defend it when their generation rises to power.

The only business specifically protected by our Constitution is the press. Our founders saw the press as an ally of the people. They believed that a free press would expose all questionable actions and policies of our leaders, regardless of their political affiliation. Unfortunately, they would be disappointed with our media today.

When the press largely ignores this noble calling and instead aligns itself with one political party or another, it gives license to that party to ignore the rule of law without fear of exposure or questions. This eventually leads to the erosion of trust and freedom. We can all hope and pray that at some point the majority of members of the press will once again align themselves with the interests of the American people and reject partisan politics and manipulation. Our nation needs a free and unbiased press.

Finally, the First Amendment addresses the right of Americans to assemble. Some societies do not allow their citizens to assemble and peacefully protest governmental policies because the governments are afraid of being overthrown. Our founders wanted to ensure the rights of citizens to gather for any reason, as long as they did it in a peaceful manner. They were not fearful of criticism and actually wanted to hear the thoughts of all of the constituents of the union. This freedom to assemble and express grievances has served as an outlet for unrest and as an effective way of requesting change. As a result, we have had hundreds of years of relative domestic peace.

It should be noted that there is a significant difference between peaceful assembly and assembling to incite rioting and violence. The latter is not protected by the Bill of Rights, nor should it be. We are a country under the rule of law, and if we fail to uphold those laws, lawlessness will increase and freedom will decrease. The purpose of the First Amendment was to increase freedom, not to decrease it, and we must keep that in mind as we consider how to uphold it.

SECOND AMENDMENT

A well regulated Militia, being necessary to the security of a free State, the right of the people to keep and bear Arms, shall not be infringed.

Our founders wanted us to have a strong national military, but they also wanted the citizens of each state to have the right to own and keep arms. In case of invasion, the populace would be able to aid our national military, and being armed would enable them to defend themselves, their families, and their property from violent criminals. To this end, the National Guard in each state is composed of its citizens and is under the control of the governor of the state. These National Guard units are under the ultimate control of the federal government, and their members can be pressed into service in the United States military.

Perhaps of even greater importance is the right of individual American citizens to own and maintain any legal arms that they can purchase or obtain. The founders knew that tyranny was often preceded by the confiscation of weapons from the citizenry. They felt confident that good leaders were in place at the time that our Constitution was formulated, but they were not certain that a time in the future might not produce leaders with a different vision of what America should be, who might use force to bend America to their own will. If that happened, the founders wanted the American people to be able to fight for their freedom and for the values and principles that established our nation. They knew that this kind of uprising would not be possible unless the people were able to own and keep arms.

This right can in no way be violated, and any attempt to erode it should be vigorously resisted. Those who insist that tyranny could never come to America should read about how it came to so many other places that also felt safe. No one ever expects tyranny, but wise men will always be prepared for it.

Many Americans who are antigun are good people with good hearts and are concerned about the safety of children and all citizens. Unfortunately, too often they are narrowly focused on their primary concern and simply cannot imagine a situation where American citizens would have to physically fight for their freedom. They would likely learn the importance of the Second Amendment only after their freedoms had been lost.

Those who do understand the importance of this amendment should make every attempt to be sensitive to the concerns of those who are frightened by guns and violence. There is nothing to be lost by engaging in rational conversations about how to quell gun violence. There are many reasonable ways to reduce violent crime without compromising the integrity of the Second Amendment. At all costs, however, we must uphold the rights of the citizens to have and bear arms.

THIRD AMENDMENT

No Soldier shall, in time of peace be quartered in any house, without the consent of the Owner; nor in time of war, but in a manner to be prescribed by law.

This amendment was a direct result of the resentment that Americans had felt when British soldiers invaded the homes of Americans during the revolution. The British government gave its soldiers the authority to demand that the colonists feed them and provide them with sleeping quarters. In many cases the soldiers abused this privilege. Our Congress wanted to be sure that this never happened again except in extraordinary cases of war with government oversight.

FOURTH AMENDMENT

The right of the people to be secure in their persons, houses, papers, and effects, against unreasonable searches and seizures, shall not be violated, and no Warrants shall issue, but upon probable cause, supported by Oath or affirmation, and particularly describing the place to be searched, and the persons or things to be seized.

This amendment protects our right of privacy. In America no authority has the right to search your private properties or information without just cause. If the authorities suspect criminal activity, they are required to obtain a search warrant from a judicial authority before conducting a search. Without this kind of protection, any citizen could be mercilessly harassed at any time of the day or night, and no one would be entitled to privacy in their lives.

This is one of the reasons why so many people were alarmed when it was discovered that the National Security Agency (NSA) was surreptitiously collecting private information about random American citizens in an attempt to thwart terrorist plots. This would perhaps be less concerning if everyone trusted the government to be honest in all of its dealings with citizens. However, situations like the scandal about a government agency (the IRS) being used to persecute political foes do much to erode such confidence.

As technological advances occur, wise leaders will need to continue to study the Fourth Amendment and consider how it should be applied to these ever-more-sophisticated technological advances. We no longer live in the age of papers and books alone; rather, we have advanced into the cyber age. This means that much of our private information can be hacked or monitored by external forces, including governmental agencies, without our knowledge. I am virtually certain that our founders would not have approved of the random monitoring of private information that is possible in cyberspace.

Of course, the excuse is given that the government has to perform random monitoring to decrease the chances of successful attacks by terrorists. We have been repeatedly assured that safeguards are in place to prevent abuse of the information gathered about innocent citizens. That would perhaps be more comforting if there had not been so many instances of inappropriate secrecy and dishonesty recently by agents of the federal government.

The wonderful thing about our system is that we have the ability, through judicial review and the establishment of a legal precedent or by constitutional amendment, to rectify the situation. In case anyone fears that government authorities will be kept from getting information they need, it should be pointed out that officials can readily obtain the necessary search warrants if they have a legitimate suspicion about one of our citizens. There is never a good reason for indiscriminate violation of privacy. If we are to remain free, we must be vigilant about protecting our liberties, not quick to give them up for the sake of security.

FIFTH AMENDMENT

No person shall be held to answer for a capital, or other infamous crime, unless on a presentment or indictment of a Grand Jury, except in cases arising in the land or naval forces, or in the Militia, when in actual service in time of War or public danger; nor shall any person be subject for the same offence to be twice put in jeopardy of life or limb; nor shall be compelled in any criminal case to be a witness against himself, nor be deprived of life, liberty, or property, without due process of law; nor shall private property be taken for public use, without just compensation.

The Fifth Amendment prohibits the authorities from taking your life, liberty, or property in an arbitrary manner. First this amendment protects American citizens accused of serious crimes from being tried in a court of law by our government without first being indicted by a grand jury. A grand jury reviews the evidence in the case and decides if there is enough evidence to bring charges. This prevents the government from arbitrarily putting people in prison or executing citizens without due process.

This amendment also includes the "double jeopardy" clause frequently quoted by legal authorities. This clause declares that a citizen cannot be tried again for the same crime if he was found not guilty the first time. There are exceptions to the rule and a number of legal maneuvers that can allow prosecutors to go after criminals who have beat the system, but the rule is really there to prevent the government from harassing people endlessly.

When defendants say, "I'm pleading the fifth," they are referring to the portion of the Fifth Amendment that says you cannot be forced to testify against yourself. This makes forced confessions, torture, blackmail, and a host of other unsavory tactics less likely to be used by prosecutors and law-enforcement agents.

Finally, the Fifth Amendment prevents the government from confiscating private property that is needed for governmental purposes without fairly compensating the citizen who owns the property. Many emotional disputes between the government and citizens arise because the government feels that it needs someone's property to initiate or complete a project. Sometimes that property has been in a family for many generations and is worth far more to the family than it is to the government. If the government can demonstrate that the property is needed for the public good and provides fair compensation, the property owner has no recourse.

SIXTH AMENDMENT

In all criminal prosecutions, the accused shall enjoy the right to a speedy and public trial, by an impartial jury of the State and district wherein the crime shall have been committed, which district shall have been previously ascertained by law, and to be informed of the nature and cause of the accusation; to be confronted with the witnesses against him; to have compulsory process for obtaining witnesses in his favor, and to have the Assistance of Counsel for his defence.

This amendment governs the way a defendant is tried. It ensures that people do not languish in jail for extended periods of time while awaiting trial. The amendment states that the defendant is entitled to a trial by jury and that the jury must be from the area in which the crime was committed. Furthermore, the person being tried must be provided with information about the accusations against him so he can form a defense. If the defendant cannot afford a lawyer, the government must provide one, and if necessary the court is to use its power to compel defense witnesses to come to court. We should be thankful that we live in a land where the government is required to work so hard to protect the rights of the accused.

SEVENTH AMENDMENT

In Suits at common law, where the value in controversy shall exceed twenty dollars, the right of trial by jury shall be preserved, and no fact tried by a jury, shall be otherwise re-examined in any Court of the United States, than according to the rules of the common law.

The Seventh Amendment governs the majority of court cases in America, which are civil cases, not criminal cases. These cases can be tried by a judge or by a jury. When money is at issue, cases of low value are generally tried by a judge, because the amounts at stake do not justify the expense of assembling a jury.

Cases tried in a lower court cannot be overturned by a higher court unless there is evidence that the applicable law was misapplied by the lower court or that the lower court's decision was inappropriate for a variety of other reasons.

EIGHTH AMENDMENT

> Excessive bail shall not be required, nor excessive fines imposed, nor cruel and unusual punishments inflicted.

This provision protects citizens from judges who might set bail in an amount far beyond what is reasonable or possible for the defendant to pay. An unfair judge might also be tempted to impose excessive fines in order to cripple a person financially. This amendment prevents that kind of abuse.

The Eighth Amendment also protects against physical abuse. Almost every American knows that our system protects us against cruel and unusual punishment. That means authorities are not allowed to use torture or "creative" forms of punishment. Even individuals who have committed capital crimes and have been given the death penalty are entitled to death in a manner that does not produce excessive pain or suffering, even though many might want to see them suffer greatly.

NINTH AMENDMENT

The enumeration in the Constitution, of certain rights, shall not be construed to deny or disparage others retained by the people.

The writers of the Constitution were well aware of the fact that they could not possibly list every important citizens' right that might need to be considered in the future. For this reason they included the Ninth Amendment, which states that just because a right is not covered in the Constitution or Bill of Rights does not mean the right is invalid.

TENTH AMENDMENT

The powers not delegated to the United States by the Constitution, not prohibited by it to the States, are reserved to the States respectively, or to the people.

The Tenth Amendment is there to help the federal government keep itself in perspective. It reminds the three branches of our federal government that they have specific enumerated powers and that they are not allowed to arbitrarily usurp the powers vested in the state governments. If the Constitution does not list a certain power as belonging to the federal government, that power belongs to the states or to the people.

By emphasizing the power of the states in this amendment, our founders hoped to keep the size and power of the federal government under control while enhancing the individuality and power of each state. Each of our fifty states has its own unique characteristics, and people reside in a given state because they enjoy the atmosphere and the camaraderie of like-minded people. The individuality of our states is immensely valuable and provides a host of options for all of our citizens, who can freely move to any state of their choice. If the federal government becomes too dominant, it will try to create uniformity to make domination of the people much easier. This amendment prevents that kind of power grab.

This amendment also recognizes that significant power should remain in the hands of the people. In some cases states initiate ballot referenda, putting controversial issues up for a vote so that the people can decide. In recent years some federal judges have taken it upon themselves to overrule the will of the people, changing or negating the outcomes of their votes in some cases. They will continue to do this and may even become more aggressive if their power is not challenged by the people through their congressional representatives.

There will likely always be tension among the federal government, the state government, and the people. This is probably healthy and was anticipated by the founders, who tried to establish a balance of power between the federal government and the states.

GOING FORWARD

The Bill of Rights was ratified in 1791 in response to fears of the Anti-Federalists that the central government would become too powerful and usurp the rights of the people. As long as we the people know and exercise our rights, we will always maintain our freedom. We must never allow ourselves to be silenced by law or by things like political correctness or other social pressures, for it is open discussion that upholds our Bill of Rights and allows progress in a pluralistic society.

CHAPTER 14
LATER AMENDMENTS

*"Joyful is the person who finds wisdom, the one who
gains understanding. For wisdom is more profitable than
silver, and her wages are better than gold."*

Proverbs 3:13–14

In medicine we frequently use the initials *prn*, short for the
Latin *pro re nata*, or "as the situation demands." All of the
amendments added after the Bill of Rights are *prn*. As the nation
has faced new challenges not sufficiently addressed in the Constitution, legislators have used the constitutional amendment
process to rectify the problems as the changing times required.

ELEVENTH AMENDMENT

The Judicial power of the United States shall not be
construed to extend to any suit in law or equity, commenced or prosecuted against one of the United
States by Citizens of another State, or by Citizens or
Subjects of any Foreign State.

This amendment was added to clarify the role of the federal courts in interstate disputes. Many felt that disputes

between entities in different states should be settled in the federal courts. As the United States grew in size and complexity, such an arrangement would have overwhelmed the federal court system. The Eleventh Amendment makes it clear that persons or entities that are foreign to a state or to our nation are not entitled to use the federal court system to sue that state or our nation. They may bring such a lawsuit only in state court in the state where the alleged infraction or injury occurred.

TWELFTH AMENDMENT

The Twelfth Amendment is lengthy and provides the nuts and bolts of how the Electoral College operates in presidential elections. The electoral process, covered in an earlier chapter, was convoluted and deeply confusing before this amendment improved the process. This amendment did away with the system of the president and vice president being the two candidates with the most votes, because it had become apparent that two rivals were not the best team. This amendment also makes it clear that the vice president must have the same qualifications as the president, which makes sense, given that the president could become incapacitated or die at any time and the vice president would have to take his place.

There are many who are unhappy with the existence of the Electoral College and would prefer to have the presidential election decided by popular vote. There are a couple of historical instances where this would have resulted in the election of a different president. This topic warrants further discussion, because circumstances have changed significantly in this country since the Electoral College system was established.

THIRTEENTH AMENDMENT

Neither slavery nor involuntary servitude, except as a punishment for crime whereof the party shall have been duly convicted, shall exist within the United States, or any place subject to their jurisdiction.

Congress shall have power to enforce this article by appropriate legislation.

The Thirteenth Amendment ended slavery and involuntary servitude in the United States and all of its territories. Many other nations, including England, had already ended slavery several years earlier, but it took a civil war to end slavery in America, because it was a huge part of our economic strength. This amendment also gave the federal government the power to ensure that involuntary servitude of any type never returned, with the exception of forced labor by convicted criminals.

The sex-slavery industry that operates in America today is clearly in violation of the Constitution. Those who force children into onerous uncompensated labor are also on unconstitutional ground under this amendment. These activities are clearly immoral and illegal, and we must work to see that they are eliminated.

FOURTEENTH AMENDMENT

All persons born or naturalized in the United States, and subject to the jurisdiction thereof, are citizens of the United States and of the state wherein they reside. No State shall make or enforce any law which shall abridge the privileges or immunities of citizens of the United States; nor shall any State deprive any person of life, liberty, or property, without due process of law; nor deny to any person within its jurisdiction the equal protection of the laws.

Under this amendment a child born in the United States is a citizen of the United States even if the child's parents are not citizens. In many countries of the world this is not the case, but at the time we enacted this law, we were trying to attract more citizens to build up our population.

This amendment was actually designed to establish and preserve the rights of former slaves as full-fledged citizens of the United States. After the slaves were emancipated, some officials tried to relegate former slaves to a status inferior to that of ordinary citizens. Unfortunately, many of these immoral people were able to get away with their cruel acts and decrees, but at least such efforts were made illegal by this amendment.

This amendment also prevents states from infringing the right of any United States citizen to life, liberty, or property. Without these kinds of specifically enumerated rights for citizens, rogue judges and other civil authorities could enrich themselves at the expense of their fellow citizens.

This amendment also requires that all United States citizens be treated equally. This means no one group should be favored over another and laws must be applied equally to everyone. When leaders from any party decide on their own which laws to enforce and which to ignore, they are in danger of constitutional violations.

Representatives shall be apportioned among the several States according to their respective numbers, counting the whole number of persons in each State, excluding Indians not taxed. But when the right to vote at any election for the choice of electors for President and Vice-President of the United States, Representatives in Congress, the Executive and Judicial officers of a State, or the members of the Legislature thereof, is denied to any of the male inhabitants of such State, being twenty-one years of age, and citizens of the United States, or in any way abridged, except for participation in rebellion, or other crime, the basis of representation therein shall be reduced in the proportion which the number of such male citizens shall bear to the whole number of male citizens twenty-one years of age in such State.

This amendment is a prime example of legal maneuvering to prevent exploitation of former slaves. The Northerners knew that the Southern Democrats would likely try to deny the freed slaves the fair opportunity to vote. Part of the rationale for the formation of the Republican Party was the abolition of slavery. The Republicans were also active in trying to protect the rights of freed slaves. The Democrats, recognizing that the Northern Republicans were much more likely than they to attract the votes of the former slaves, feared losing power. By penalizing the Southern Democrats for fraudulent voting maneuvers, this amendment diminished some of the unfair activity.

> No person shall be a Senator or Representative in Congress, or elector of President and Vice-President, or hold any office, civil or military, under the United States, or under any State, who, having previously taken an oath, as a member of Congress, or as an officer of the United States, or as a member of any State legislature, or as an executive or judicial officer of any State, to support the Constitution of the United States, shall have engaged in insurrection or rebellion against the same, or given aid or comfort to the enemies thereof. But Congress may by a vote of two-thirds of each House, remove such disability.

This amendment was strictly a punitive measure to ensure that officials who had sworn allegiance to the Constitution but then joined the Confederacy would not again be able to hold public office. It remains relevant today, because there are American citizens who are joining terrorist groups that are considered enemies of America. Some of them have been captured and others will be captured later. This amendment precludes them from important public service without exceptional action by Congress.

> The validity of the public debt of the United States, authorized by law, including debts incurred for payment of pensions and bounties for services in sup-

pressing insurrection or rebellion, shall not be questioned. But neither the United States nor any State shall assume or pay any debt or obligation incurred in aid of insurrection or rebellion against the United States, or any claim for the loss or emancipation of any slave; but all such debts, obligations and claims shall be held illegal and void.

The Congress shall have power to enforce, by appropriate legislation, the provisions of this article.

Substantial debts were incurred by both sides during the Civil War. Clearly everyone wanted to be repaid for loans they had made to the federal government, and this law allowed the federal government to pay Union debts while essentially declaring Confederate debts nonpayable. This and other governmental actions severely hampered any actions on behalf of the Southern slave owners to reestablish power through financial strength.

Unfortunately, this amendment has been used as justification of expanding federal debt without need for explanation. It is unlikely that the authors of this amendment knew that it would eventually result in the potential bankruptcy of the nation.

FIFTEENTH AMENDMENT

The right of the citizens of the United States to vote shall not be denied or abridged by the United States or by any State on account of race, color, or previous condition of servitude.

The Congress shall have power to enforce this article by appropriate legislation.

The Fourteenth Amendment established that former slaves born in the United States would be citizens of the United States, but Southern Democrats were adamantly opposed to allowing their former slaves to be equal to them in civic power. They attempted to use legal maneuvers to circumvent the Fourteenth Amendment and obliterate the voting rights of black men. The Fifteenth Amendment was necessary to protect the rights of these new voters.

It is easy for us today to criticize those self-centered individuals in the past who tried to disenfranchise the freedmen. Unfortunately, our society is still plagued by people who propose and enforce policies that encourage the descendants of the freedmen to accept a state of social dependency. People in such a state tend to be much easier to manipulate than people who are independent and well educated. Therefore, with a few perks and promises, their votes can be cultivated, creating a significant power base. Manipulative people convince them that others are responsible for their misery and that they should be grateful for the aid being provided by their saviors.

There are others on the other side of the political spectrum, although few in number, who try to disenfranchise minority voters by putting obstacles in their way. As a society we must always do all that we can to ensure the voting rights of every citizen.

SIXTEENTH AMENDMENT

The Congress shall have power to lay and collect taxes on incomes, from whatever source derived, without apportionment among the several States, and without regard to any census or enumeration.

It would be difficult to operate the federal government without a steady and dependable source of income. The Sixteenth Amendment was passed to ensure that the federal government could tax virtually any source of income within the United States in order to meet its fiscal obligations. Prior to its passage, a hodgepodge of methods were used to collect money from citizens for the purpose of running the government. None of these worked very well. This amendment laid the groundwork for some consistency in taxation.

SEVENTEENTH AMENDMENT

The Senate of the United States shall be composed of two Senators from each State, elected by the people thereof, for six years; and each Senator shall have one vote. The electors in each state shall have the qualifications requisite for electors of the most numerous branch of the State legislatures.

When vacancies happen in the representation of any State in the Senate, the executive authority of such State shall issue writs of election to fill such vacancies: *Provided,* That the legislature of any State may empower the executive thereof to make temporary appointments until the people fill the vacancies by election as the legislature may direct.

This amendment shall not be so construed as to affect the election or term of any Senator chosen before it becomes valid as part of the Constitution.

This amendment changed the procedure for the election of senators. Over time it had become clear that having U.S.

senators be elected by their respective state legislatures increased corruption. Wealthy individuals who wanted a seat in the Senate could bribe members of the state legislatures to vote for them. To prevent the buying and selling of Senate seats, the Constitution was amended to require senators to be chosen through general elections, with interim senators to be appointed by the state's governor in cases of emergency. The new procedure decreased cronyism and increased accountability. When dependent upon the goodwill of the voters, senators became more responsive to the will of the people and represented them better.

EIGHTEENTH AMENDMENT

The Eighteenth Amendment was also known as the prohibition amendment. It prohibited the manufacture and sale of alcoholic beverages in the United States. That, of course, led to a huge black market and a massive increase in violent crime. All three sections of this amendment were repealed by the Twenty-first Amendment.

NINETEENTH AMENDMENT

The right of citizens of the United States to vote shall not be denied or abridged by the United States or by any State on account of sex.

Congress shall have power to enforce this article by appropriate legislation.

This amendment, ratified in 1920, finally gave women the right to vote in America. It is sobering to realize that the

United States of America, today a bastion of liberty and justice, was so backward in its thinking less than a century ago. Fortunately, we have made tremendous progress in political freedom for women in a relatively short period of time. But we should not rest; we should elect wise and vigilant legislators who will notice any other failures and propose appropriate remedies.

TWENTIETH AMENDMENT

Until this lengthy amendment was enacted, there was a several-month gap between the time congressmen were elected and the time they actually went to Washington to assume their responsibilities. This amendment drastically shortened the gap, resulting in greater efficiency and less chance of mischief by resentful lame-duck representatives. There had also been questions regarding the appropriate protocol in the event of the death of the president-elect or the vice president–elect. This amendment answered those questions.

TWENTY-FIRST AMENDMENT

The eighteenth article of amendment to the Constitution of the United States is hereby repealed.

The transportation or importation into any State, Territory, or possession of the United States for delivery or use therein of intoxicating liquors, in violation of the laws thereof, is hereby prohibited.

This article shall be inoperative unless it shall have been ratified as an amendment to the Constitution by conventions in the several States, as provided in the Constitution, within seven years from the date of the submission hereof to the States by the Congress.

After careful consideration and much deliberation, Congress decided that it would be better to relegalize alcohol and deal with the consequences than to witness the continued escalation of violence and criminal activity caused by Prohibition. Thus this amendment repeals the Eighteenth Amendment but does allow individual states to retain or enact their own alcohol restrictions.

TWENTY-SECOND AMENDMENT

No person shall be elected to the office of the President more than twice, and no person who has held the office of President, or acted as President, for more than two years of a term to which some other person was elected President shall be elected to the office of President more than once. But this Article shall not apply to any person holding the office of President when this Article was proposed by the Congress, and shall not prevent any person who may be holding the office of President, or acting as President, during the term within which this Article becomes operative from holding the office of President or acting as President during the remainder of such term.

This Article shall be inoperative unless it shall have been ratified as an amendment to the Constitution by the legislatures of three-fourths of the several States within seven years from the date of its submission to the States by the Congress.

George Washington declined to run for a third term, setting a precedent for future executives that lasted until Franklin Delano Roosevelt.[1] The circumstances of his third election were quite unusual; the United States was on the brink of becoming heavily involved in World War II. Dire circumstances meant that there was no time for the usual massive political gamesmanship associated with a presidential election. During the war Roosevelt was elected to a fourth term, but he died shortly after the term began.

After Roosevelt's death, Americans worried that he had set a bad precedent, and Congress proposed a term-limit amendment. The amendment probably is not necessary, because we have a huge pool of talented and ambitious people in our country, but it guarantees that we will not establish a monarchy or a dynasty within the United States.

TWENTY-THIRD AMENDMENT

The District constituting the seat of Government of the United States shall appoint in such manner as the Congress may direct: A number of electors of President and Vice President equal to the whole number of Senators and Representatives in Congress to which the District would be entitled if it were a State, but in no event more than the least populous State; they shall be in addition to those appointed by the States, but they shall be considered, for the purposes of the election of President and Vice President, to be electors appointed by a State; and they shall meet in the District and perform such duties as provided by the twelfth article of amendment.

The Congress shall have power to enforce this article by appropriate legislation.

Washington, DC, became the seat of the federal government over two hundred years ago, and the controversy about voting rights for its residents has raged ever since. This amendment, passed in 1960, finally put the issue to rest. The city now has a number of electors, chosen on the same basis as the states' electors, who can vote in presidential elections.

Today Washington, DC, does not have senators or representatives in the House, much to the frustration of the city's population. One possible solution would be to allow the residents of Washington, DC, to affiliate themselves with either the state of Maryland or the state of Virginia. That would at least give them an opportunity to be represented in the same way as citizens in every state. A resolution has been proposed to provide DC residents with appropriate national representation; if passed, it will be the first amendment to the Constitution in over twenty years.

Since Washington, DC, is not a state, there is no state legislature to provide governance. Instead, Congress acts for Washington, DC, in the same way state legislatures do for each of the fifty states. Many DC residents are not happy with this arrangement, because they have little or no influence on the members of Congress, whereas residents of each of the fifty states can elect or dismiss their state legislators as they please. This is one of the reasons why some are advocating statehood for the District of Columbia. This would be incredibly complex and so far seems to be beyond the realm of things Congress is willing to seriously consider. Nevertheless, we must recognize that the people who live in Washington, DC, are American citizens, and we should diligently search for a way to make sure that they are empowered like everyone else.

TWENTY-FOURTH AMENDMENT

The right of citizens of the United States to vote in any primary or other election for President or Vice President, for electors for President or Vice President, or for Senator or Representative in Congress, shall not be denied or abridged by the United States or any State by reason of failure to pay any poll tax or other tax.

The Congress shall have power to enforce this article by appropriate legislation.

This amendment, ratified in 1964, abolished poll taxes, the fees voters were required to pay before filling out a ballot. Poll taxes were established in many Southern states long before slavery ended, but once blacks gained the right to vote, they were used extensively in many of the former slave states to disenfranchise black voters. Poll taxes created an economic barrier that hurt all people with low incomes but inflicted disproportional hardship on black people because of their economic position in society. Fortunately, this scheme was exposed and was turned aside by the Twenty-fourth Amendment.

Over the years, courts have broadly interpreted the Twenty-fourth Amendment to preclude the use of unusual residency requirements, literacy tests, and other arbitrary barriers to obstruct voting. Any trickery depriving American citizens of their constitutional right to vote should be exposed and vigorously opposed. In recent years, though, some have suggested that voter-identification requirements are a new version of poll taxes. This suggestion is absurd and an abuse of the amendment.

Those who feel that voter identification is not necessary have probably not taken the time to consider how valuable each vote is. In our society, identification is required for most high-value transactions. Why should voting be different? If voters don't need identification in order to vote, our elections risk voter fraud.

Every other nation to which I have traveled recently requires some type of official voter identification. I hope that we can convince the enemies of voter-identification laws that their energy currently spent fighting common sense is best spent helping disenfranchised individuals acquire the necessary identification and register to vote.

This amendment also mentions the right of citizens to vote in party primaries. In many states that right is not extended to people who are registered as independents. Other states have open primaries where members of a party can vote in the opposing party's primary, a situation that can invite unethical mischief. For example, during the Republican primary, Democrats could cross over and vote for the candidate they believe most likely to lose in the general election. This is an area that needs to be studied and addressed by legislators. There should be no incentives for dishonesty built into our electoral process, and cheating should be a federal crime, because the stakes are high.

TWENTY-FIFTH AMENDMENT

This lengthy amendment clarifies matters of presidential succession. The topic is covered in Article 2, but the original language was subject to a wide range of interpretations and needed clarification. Before this amendment was passed, presidents and vice presidents made their own informal agreements about how to manage succession and temporary power shifts. This amendment conclusively established the order of presidential succession—from the vice president to the Speaker of the House to the president pro tempore of the Senate, down through all the cabinet members until the last one, the secretary of homeland security—and standardizing the procedures was a wise move.

No sitting president has died in the past fifty years, so we rarely think about presidential succession, but it is more important than ever before. In the age of terrorist threats, we need well-defined succession plans that can be immediately implemented should the unthinkable happen.

TWENTY-SIXTH AMENDMENT

The right of citizens of the United States, who are eighteen years of age or older, to vote shall not be denied or abridged by the United States or by any State on account of age.

The Congress shall have power to enforce this article by appropriate legislation.

Since the American Revolution, teenagers and young adults have fought for freedom on the battlefields of America. Nathan

Hale began spying for the Americans when he was twenty years old and became an American hero when he was executed by the British. Before his death, he famously said, "I only regret that I have but one life to lose for my country." And yet, under the original Constitution, Hale the young spy would have been too young to vote.

Until the Twenty-sixth Amendment was passed in 1971, it was possible for young people to join the military and be injured or killed without having the right to vote. This injustice was so clear that the amendment was ratified within a mere three and a half months after Congress proposed it. The measure did not pass without debate; some states wanted to keep the age of majority at twenty-one in state elections while allowing those aged eighteen years or older to vote in federal elections. This would have been permissible, but states would have been required to have two separate voting systems, a daunting task that no state wanted to take on.

Recently there have been some challenges to the rights of college students to vote. Many students live far from home and face a dilemma—they cannot travel home to vote but cannot register in their college towns. Fortunately, the courts have ruled in favor of those students, declaring that restriction of student voting on this basis is a violation of the Twenty-sixth Amendment. Students may either vote in their college towns or use absentee ballots to vote back home.

It is more important than ever that young people become deeply involved in the political process and exercise their constitutional voting rights. It is their future that is being jeopardized by massive federal debt and inattention to foreign threats. They must recognize that the political establishment will not serve them unless they make the power of their votes felt.

TWENTY-SEVENTH AMENDMENT

No law, varying the compensation for the services of the Senators and Representatives, shall take effect, until an election of Representatives shall have intervened.

The last constitutional amendment, as of the writing of this book, was actually first proposed in 1789 by James Madison. To his disappointment, it did not receive approval of three quarters of the states and therefore was not ratified. It remained dormant for over two hundred years before finally being ratified in 1992.

Congressmen have the ability to vote on their own salaries, which of course are paid through taxes by the citizens of the United States. Many people were wary of a system that would allow the people in power to enrich themselves without oversight. This amendment provides a sensible solution to this danger. By requiring that pay raises not go into effect until after the next election, it ensures that members of Congress must face the voters for approval before receiving that salary.

Members of Congress are accordingly careful not to anger voters by paying themselves excessive salaries. Many of them, however, do not apply fiscal restraint in other areas, spending taxpayer money on pet projects and favors for special-interest groups. When they examine the records of their congressional representatives, voters must be just as careful to look for overspending as they are to look at salary increases. Increased taxation and irresponsible fiscal policies should be rewarded with removal from office by vigilant constituents. We must remember and we must remind them that it is our money they are spending.

CONCLUSION

Since the Bill of Rights was ratified, we've added only seventeen more amendments to the Constitution. The fact that our governing document has required so few adjustments in over two hundred years testifies to the brilliance of the founders. We should be grateful that they built in mechanisms for amendment, but we should also think carefully whenever new amendments are suggested. The stability of this document and the wisdom displayed within it should make us attentive to its admonitions now and in the future. Let us be quick to learn and slow to change it.

CHAPTER 15
A CALL TO ACTION

"Oh, the joys of those who do not follow the advice of the wicked, or stand around with sinners, or join in with mockers."

Psalms 1:1

When the delegates at the Constitutional Convention framed our Constitution more than two hundred years ago, they were seeking to improve on a union that was too weak. Today our challenge is to rein in a union that is growing too strong. Keeping a government restrained is hard. People always want more power, and power corrupts.

Fortunately, the Constitution's framers fully understood that it would be necessary to control the growth and power of the central government in order to maintain the freedom of its citizens. In fact, in 1799 Thomas Jefferson said, "Free government is founded in jealousy, and not in confidence. It is jealousy and not confidence which prescribes limited constitutions, to bind those whom we are obliged to trust with power. . . . In questions of power, then, let no more be heard of confidence in man, but bind him down from mischief by the chains of the Constitution."[1] He understood the nature of men and recognized the danger of entrusting them with power. John Adams said, "It is weakness rather than wickedness which renders men unfit to be trusted with unlimited power."[2]

The question today is not whether we know what's wrong with our country—we see that our government is infringing upon the rights of the populace. Nor is the question whether we have ways to solve the problem. Because of the founders' wisdom, we have all the tools we need to reduce the power of the federal government. We have legislative, judicial, and executive channels for remedying overreach. We have the means to amend the Constitution when needed. We have all the legal backup we need to stand up for the rights of the people.

The question is whether we have the courage to fill the prescription. Are we willing to stand up against the PC police? Are we willing to educate ourselves and others? We the people must be knowledgeable about our Constitution and brave enough to act upon our values, principles, and convictions.

I am encouraged that you have taken the time to read this book. As long as readers like you seek to understand and defend the Constitution, America has a chance of maintaining her greatness. Our founders depended on voters like you when they sought to form "a more perfect Union." With God's grace, they succeeded. And under His care, America's best days may still be ahead.

Thomas Paine wrote the first of his "American Crisis" articles in 1776. On Christmas Eve, Washington ordered that Paine's words be read to the troops to inspire them as they prepared to attack a much larger troop of enemy forces. The message was effective; the next day, the four thousand American soldiers surprised the twenty thousand Hessian fighters and won a victory that restored American morale.

Paine's words were written nearly 240 years ago, but they are just as compelling today as they were then:

These are the times that try men's souls. The summer soldier and the sunshine patriot will, in this crisis, shrink from the service of his country, but he that stands it NOW, deserves the love and thanks of man and woman. Tyranny, like hell, is not easily conquered; yet we have this consolation with us, that the harder the conflict, the more glorious the triumph. What we obtain too cheap, we esteem too lightly: 'tis dearness only that gives every thing its value. Heaven knows how to put a proper price upon its goods, and it would be strange indeed, if so celestial an article as FREEDOM should not be highly rated.[3]

Fellow Americans, our nation faces a new crisis today. Once again, our freedom will come at the price of courage, strength, and faith. The future is in our hands.

ACKNOWLEDGMENTS

We would like to express our sincere appreciation for the people at Sentinel who worked with us:

Adrian Zackheim, publisher

Will Weisser, associate publisher and director of marketing

Jacquelynn Burke, senior publicist

Bria Sandford, associate editor

As well as Andrea Jewell and Kris Bearss for their very timely help in the eleventh hour. And last but not least we must heartily thank Sealy Yates, whose insights and suggestions have been exceptional.

APPENDIX: THE CONSTITUTION OF THE UNITED STATES OF AMERICA

PREAMBLE

We the People of the United States, in Order to form a more perfect Union, establish Justice, insure domestic Tranquility, provide for the common defence, promote the general Welfare, and secure the Blessings of Liberty to ourselves and our Posterity, do ordain and establish this Constitution for the United States of America.

ARTICLE I

Section 1. All legislative Powers herein granted shall be vested in a Congress of the United States, which shall consist of a Senate and House of Representatives.

Section 2. The House of Representatives shall be composed of Members chosen every second Year by the People of the several States, and the Electors in each State shall have the Qualifications requisite for Electors of the most numerous Branch of the State Legislature.

No Person shall be a Representative who shall not have attained to the Age of twenty five Years, and been seven Years a Citizen of the United States, and who shall not, when elected, be an Inhabitant of that State in which he shall be chosen.

Representatives and direct Taxes shall be apportioned among the several States which may be included within this Union, according to their respective Numbers, which shall be determined by adding to the whole Number of free Persons, including those bound to Service for a Term of Years, and excluding Indians not taxed, three fifths of all other Persons. The actual Enumeration shall be made within three Years after the first Meeting of the Congress of the United States, and within every subsequent Term of ten Years, in such Manner as they shall by Law direct. The number of Representatives shall not exceed one for every thirty Thousand, but each State shall have at Least one Representative; and until such enumeration shall be made, the State of New Hampshire shall be entitled to chuse three, Massachusetts eight, Rhode-Island and Providence Plantations one, Connecticut five, New-York six, New Jersey four, Pennsylvania eight, Delaware one, Maryland six, Virginia ten, North Carolina five, South Carolina five, and Georgia three.

When vacancies happen in the Representation from any State, the Executive Authority thereof shall issue Writs of Election to fill such Vacancies.

The House of Representatives shall chuse their Speaker and other Officers; and shall have the sole Power of Impeachment.

Section 3. The Senate of the United States shall be composed of two Senators from each State, chosen by the Legislature thereof, for six Years; and each Senator shall have one Vote.

Immediately after they shall be assembled in Consequence of the first Election, they shall be divided as equally as may be into three Classes. The Seats of the Senators of the first Class shall be vacated at the Expiration of the second Year, of the second Class at the Expiration of the fourth Year, and of the third Class at the Expiration of the sixth Year, so that one third may be chosen every second Year; and if Vacancies happen by Resignation, or otherwise, during the Recess of the Legislature of any State, the Executive thereof may make temporary Appointments until the next Meeting of the Legislature, which shall then fill such Vacancies.

No Person shall be a Senator who shall not have attained to the Age of thirty Years, and been nine Years a Citizen of the United States, and who shall not, when elected, be an Inhabitant of that State for which he shall be chosen.

The Vice President of the United States shall be President of the Senate, but shall have no Vote, unless they be equally divided.

The Senate shall chuse their other Officers, and also a President pro tempore, in the Absence of the Vice President, or when he shall exercise the Office of President of the United States.

The Senate shall have the sole Power to try all Impeachments. When sitting for that Purpose, they shall be on Oath or Affirmation. When the President of the United States is tried, the Chief Justice shall preside: And no Person shall be convicted without the Concurrence of two thirds of the Members present.

Judgment in Cases of Impeachment shall not extend further than to removal from Office, and disqualification to hold and enjoy any Office of honor, Trust or Profit under the United States: but the Party convicted shall nevertheless be liable and subject to Indictment, Trial, Judgment and Punishment, according to Law.

Section 4. The Times, Places and Manner of holding Elections for Senators and Representatives, shall be prescribed in each State by the Legislature thereof; but the Congress may at any time by Law make or alter such Regulations, except as to the Places of chusing Senators.

The Congress shall assemble at least once in every Year, and such Meeting shall be on the first Monday in December, unless they shall by Law appoint a different Day.

Section 5. Each House shall be the Judge of the Elections, Returns and Qualifications of its own Members, and a Majority of each shall constitute a Quorum to do Business; but a smaller Number may adjourn from day to day, and may be authorized to compel the Attendance of absent Members, in such Manner, and under such Penalties as each House may provide.

Each House may determine the Rules of its Proceedings, punish its Members for disorderly Behaviour, and, with the Concurrence of two thirds, expel a Member.

Each House shall keep a Journal of its Proceedings, and from time to time publish the same, excepting such Parts as may in their Judgment require Secrecy; and the Yeas and Nays of the Members of either House on any question shall, at the Desire of one fifth of those Present, be entered on the Journal.

Neither House, during the Session of Congress, shall, without the Consent of the other, adjourn for more than three days, nor to any other Place than that in which the two Houses shall be sitting.

Section 6. The Senators and Representatives shall receive a Compensation for their Services, to be ascertained by Law, and paid out of the Treasury of the United States. They shall in all Cases, except Treason, Felony and Breach of the Peace, be privileged from Arrest during their Attendance at the Session of their respective Houses, and in going to and returning from the same; and for any Speech or Debate in either House, they shall not be questioned in any other Place.

No Senator or Representative shall, during the Time for which he was elected, be appointed to any civil Office under the Authority of the United States, which shall have been created, or the Emoluments whereof shall have been encreased during such time; and no Person holding any Office under the United States, shall be a Member of either House during his Continuance in Office.

Section 7. All Bills for raising Revenue shall originate in the House of Representatives; but the Senate may propose or concur with Amendments as on other Bills.

Every Bill which shall have passed the House of Representatives and the Senate, shall, before it become a Law, be presented to the President of the United States; If he approve he shall sign it, but if not he shall return it, with his Objections to that House in which it shall have originated, who shall enter the Objections at large on their Journal, and proceed to reconsider it. If after such Reconsideration two thirds of that House shall agree to pass the Bill, it shall be sent, together with the Objections, to the other House, by which it shall likewise be reconsidered, and if approved by two thirds of that House, it shall become a Law. But in all such Cases the Votes of both Houses shall be determined by Yeas and Nays, and the Names of the Persons voting for and against the Bill shall be entered on the Journal of each House respectively. If any Bill shall not be returned by the President within ten Days (Sundays excepted) after it shall have been presented to him, the Same shall be a Law, in like Manner as if he had signed it, unless the Congress by their Adjournment prevent its Return, in which Case it shall not be a Law.

Every Order, Resolution, or Vote to which the Concurrence of the Senate and House of Representatives may be necessary (except on a question of Adjournment) shall be presented to the President of the United States; and before the Same shall take Effect, shall be approved by him, or being disapproved by him, shall be repassed by two thirds of the Senate and House of Representatives, according to the Rules and Limitations prescribed in the Case of a Bill.

Section 8. The Congress shall have Power to lay and collect Taxes, Duties, Imposts and Excises, to pay the Debts and provide for the common Defence and general Welfare of the United States; but all Duties, Imposts and Excises shall be uniform throughout the United States;

To borrow Money on the credit of the United States;

To regulate Commerce with foreign Nations, and among the several States, and with the Indian Tribes;

To establish an uniform Rule of Naturalization, and uniform Laws on the subject of Bankruptcies throughout the United States;

To coin Money, regulate the Value thereof, and of foreign Coin, and fix the Standard of Weights and Measures;

To provide for the Punishment of counterfeiting the Securities and current Coin of the United States;

To establish Post Offices and post Roads;

To promote the Progress of Science and useful Arts, by securing for limited Times to Authors and Inventors the exclusive Right to their respective Writings and Discoveries;

To constitute Tribunals inferior to the supreme Court;

To define and punish Piracies and Felonies committed on the high Seas, and Offenses against the Law of Nations;

To declare War, grant Letters of Marque and Reprisal, and make Rules concerning Captures on Land and Water;

To raise and support Armies, but no Appropriation of Money to that Use shall be for a longer Term than two Years;

To provide and maintain a Navy;

To make Rules for the Government and Regulation of the land and naval Forces;

To provide for calling forth the Militia to execute the Laws of the Union, suppress Insurrections and repel Invasions;

To provide for organizing, arming, and disciplining, the Militia, and for governing such Part of them as may be employed in the Service of the United States, reserving to the States respectively, the Appointment of the Officers, and the Authority of training the Militia according to the discipline prescribed by Congress;

To exercise exclusive Legislation in all Cases whatsoever, over such District (not exceeding ten Miles square) as may, by Cession of particular States, and the Acceptance of Congress, become the Seat of the Government of the United States, and to exercise like Authority over all Places purchased by the Consent of the Legislature of the State in which the Same shall be, for the Erection of Forts, Magazines, Arsenals, dock-Yards and other needful Buildings;—And

To make all Laws which shall be necessary and proper for carrying into Execution the foregoing Powers, and all other Powers vested by this Constitution in the Government of the United States, or in any Department or Officer thereof.

Section 9. The Migration or Importation of such Persons as any of the States now existing shall think proper to admit, shall not be prohibited by the Congress prior to the Year one thousand eight hundred and eight, but a Tax or duty may be imposed on such Importation, not exceeding ten dollars for each Person.

The Privilege of the Writ of Habeas Corpus shall not be suspended, unless when in Cases of Rebellion or Invasion the public Safety may require it.

No Bill of Attainder or ex post facto Law shall be passed.

No Capitation, or other direct, Tax shall be laid, unless in Proportion to the Census or enumeration herein before directed to be taken.

No Tax or Duty shall be laid on Articles exported from any State.

No Preference shall be given by any Regulation of Commerce or Revenue to the Ports of one State over those of another: nor shall Vessels bound to, or from, one State, be obliged to enter, clear, or pay Duties in another.

No Money shall be drawn from the Treasury, but in Consequence of Appropriations made by Law; and a regular Statement and Account of the Receipts and Expenditures of all public Money shall be published from time to time.

No Title of Nobility shall be granted by the United States: And no Person holding any Office of Profit or Trust under them, shall, without the Consent of the Congress, accept of any present, Emolument, Office, or Title, of any kind whatever, from any King, Prince, or foreign State.

Section 10. No State shall enter into any Treaty, Alliance, or Confederation; grant Letters of Marque and Reprisal; coin

Money; emit Bills of Credit; make any Thing but gold and silver Coin a Tender in Payment of Debts; pass any Bill of Attainder, ex post facto Law, or Law impairing the Obligation of Contracts, or grant any Title of Nobility.

No State shall, without the Consent of the Congress, lay any Imposts or Duties on Imports or Exports, except what may be absolutely necessary for executing it's inspection Laws: and the net Produce of all Duties and Imposts, laid by any State on Imports or Exports, shall be for the Use of the Treasury of the United States; and all such Laws shall be subject to the Revision and Controul of the Congress.

No State shall, without the Consent of Congress, lay any Duty of Tonnage, keep Troops, or Ships of War in time of Peace, enter into any Agreement or Compact with another State, or with a foreign Power, or engage in War, unless actually invaded, or in such imminent Danger as will not admit of delay.

ARTICLE II

Section 1. The executive Power shall be vested in a President of the United States of America. He shall hold his Office during the Term of four Years, and, together with the Vice President, chosen for the same Term, be elected, as follows:

Each State shall appoint, in such Manner as the Legislature thereof may direct, a Number of Electors, equal to the whole Number of Senators and Representatives to which the State may be entitled in the Congress: but no Senator or Representative, or Person holding an Office of Trust or Profit under the United States, shall be appointed an Elector.

The Electors shall meet in their respective States, and

vote by Ballot for two Persons, of whom one at least shall not be an Inhabitant of the same State with themselves. And they shall make a List of all the Persons voted for, and of the Number of Votes for each; which List they shall sign and certify, and transmit sealed to the Seat of the Government of the United States, directed to the President of the Senate. The President of the Senate shall, in the Presence of the Senate and House of Representatives, open all the Certificates, and the Votes shall then be counted. The Person having the greatest Number of Votes shall be the President, if such Number be a Majority of the whole Number of Electors appointed; and if there be more than one who have such Majority, and have an equal Number of Votes, then the House of Representatives shall immediately chuse by Ballot one of them for President; and if no Person have a Majority, then from the five highest on the List the said House shall in like Manner chuse the President. But in chusing the President, the Votes shall be taken by States, the Representation from each State having one Vote; A quorum for this Purpose shall consist of a Member or Members from two thirds of the States, and a Majority of all the States shall be necessary to a Choice. In every Case, after the Choice of the President, the Person having the greatest Number of Votes of the Electors shall be the Vice President. But if there should remain two or more who have equal Votes, the Senate shall chuse from them by Ballot the Vice President.

The Congress may determine the Time of chusing the Electors, and the Day on which they shall give their Votes; which Day shall be the same throughout the United States.

No Person except a natural born Citizen, or a Citizen of

the United States, at the time of the Adoption of this Constitution, shall be eligible to the Office of President; neither shall any person be eligible to that Office who shall not have attained to the Age of thirty five Years, and been fourteen Years a Resident within the United States.

In Case of the Removal of the President from Office, or of his Death, Resignation, or Inability to discharge the Powers and Duties of the said Office, the Same shall devolve on the Vice President, and the Congress may by Law provide for the Case of Removal, Death, Resignation or Inability, both of the President and Vice President, declaring what Officer shall then act as President, and such Officer shall act accordingly, until the Disability be removed, or a President shall be elected.

The President shall, at stated Times, receive for his Services, a Compensation, which shall neither be encreased nor diminished during the Period for which he shall have been elected, and he shall not receive within that Period any other Emolument from the United States, or any of them.

Before he enter on the Execution of his Office, he shall take the following Oath or Affirmation:—"I do solemnly swear (or affirm) that I will faithfully execute the Office of President of the United States, and will to the best of my Ability, preserve, protect and defend the Constitution of the United States."

Section 2. The President shall be Commander in Chief of the Army and Navy of the United States, and of the Militia of the several States, when called into the actual Service of the United States; he may require the Opinion, in writing, of the principal Officer in each of the executive Departments, upon any Subject relating to the Duties of their respective Offices, and he shall have Power to grant Reprieves and Pardons for Offences against the United States, except in Cases of Impeachment.

He shall have Power, by and with the Advice and Consent of the Senate, to make Treaties, provided two thirds of the Senators present concur; and he shall nominate, and by and with the Advice and Consent of the Senate, shall appoint Ambassadors, other public Ministers and Consuls, Judges of the supreme Court, and all other Officers of the United States, whose Appointments are not herein otherwise provided for, and which shall be established by Law: but the Congress may by Law vest the Appointment of such inferior Officers, as they think proper, in the President alone, in the Courts of Law, or in the Heads of Departments.

The President shall have Power to fill up all Vacancies that may happen during the Recess of the Senate, by granting Commissions which shall expire at the End of their next Session.

Section 3. He shall from time to time give to the Congress Information of the State of the Union, and recommend to their Consideration such Measures as he shall judge necessary and expedient; he may, on extraordinary Occasions, convene both Houses, or either of them, and in Case of Disagreement between them, with Respect to the Time of Adjournment, he may adjourn them to such Time as he shall think proper; he shall receive Ambassadors and other public Ministers; he shall take Care that the Laws be faithfully executed, and shall Commission all the Officers of the United States.

Section 4. The President, Vice President and all civil Officers of the United States, shall be removed from Office on Impeachment for, and Conviction of, Treason, Bribery, or other high Crimes and Misdemeanors.

ARTICLE III

Section 1. The judicial Power of the United States, shall be vested in one supreme Court, and in such inferior Courts as the Congress may from time to time ordain and establish. The Judges, both of the supreme and inferior Courts, shall hold their Offices during good Behaviour, and shall, at stated Times, receive for their Services, a Compensation, which shall not be diminished during their Continuance in Office.

Section 2. The judicial Power shall extend to all Cases, in Law and Equity, arising under this Constitution, the Laws of the United States, and Treaties made, or which shall be made, under their Authority;—to all Cases affecting Ambassadors, other public Ministers and Consuls;—to all Cases of admiralty and maritime Jurisdiction;—to Controversies to which the United States shall be a Party;—to Controversies between two or more States;—between a State and Citizens of another State;—between Citizens of different States;—between Citizens of the same State claiming Lands under Grants of different States, and between a State, or the Citizens thereof, and foreign States, Citizens or Subjects.

In all Cases affecting Ambassadors, other public Ministers and Consuls, and those in which a State shall be Party, the supreme Court shall have original Jurisdiction. In all the other Cases before mentioned, the supreme Court shall have appellate Jurisdiction, both as to Law and Fact, with such Exceptions, and under such Regulations as the Congress shall make.

The Trial of all Crimes, except in Cases of Impeachment; shall be by Jury; and such Trial shall be held in the State where the said Crimes shall have been committed; but when not committed within any State, the Trial shall be at such Place or Places as the Congress may by Law have directed.

Section 3. Treason against the United States, shall consist only in levying War against them, or in adhering to their Enemies, giving them Aid and Comfort. No Person shall be convicted of Treason unless on the Testimony of two Witnesses to the same overt Act, or on Confession in open Court.

The Congress shall have Power to declare the Punishment of Treason, but no Attainder of Treason shall work Corruption of Blood, or Forfeiture except during the Life of the Person attainted.

ARTICLE IV

Section 1. Full Faith and Credit shall be given in each State to the public Acts, Records, and judicial Proceedings of every other State. And the Congress may by general Laws prescribe the Manner in which such Acts, Records and Proceedings shall be proved, and the Effect thereof.

Section 2. The Citizens of each State shall be entitled to all Privileges and Immunities of Citizens in the several States.

A Person charged in any State with Treason, Felony, or other Crime, who shall flee from Justice, and be found in another State, shall on Demand of the executive Authority of the State from which he fled, be delivered up, to be removed to the State having Jurisdiction of the Crime.

No Person held to Service or Labour in one State, under the Laws thereof, escaping into another, shall, in Consequence of any Law or Regulation therein, be discharged from such Service or Labour, but shall be delivered up on Claim of the Party to whom such Service or Labour may be due.

Section 3. New States may be admitted by the Congress into this Union; but no new State shall be formed or erected within the Jurisdiction of any other State; nor any State be formed by the Junction of two or more States, or Parts of States, without the Consent of the Legislatures of the States concerned as well as of the Congress.

The Congress shall have Power to dispose of and make all needful Rules and Regulations respecting the Territory or other Property belonging to the United States; and nothing in this Constitution shall be so construed as to Prejudice any Claims of the United States, or of any particular State.

Section 4. The United States shall guarantee to every State in this Union a Republican Form of Government, and shall protect each of them against Invasion; and on Application of the Legislature, or of the Executive (when the Legislature cannot be convened), against domestic Violence.

ARTICLE V

The Congress, whenever two thirds of both Houses shall deem it necessary, shall propose Amendments to this Constitution, or, on the Application of the Legislatures of two thirds of the several States, shall call a Convention for proposing Amendments, which, in either Case, shall be valid to all Intents and Purposes, as Part of this Constitution, when ratified by the Legislatures of three fourths of the several States, or by Conventions in three fourths thereof, as the one or the other Mode of Ratification may be proposed by the Congress; Provided that no Amendment which may be made prior to the Year One thousand eight hundred and eight shall in any Manner affect the first and fourth Clauses in the Ninth Section of the first Article; and that no State, without its Consent, shall be deprived of its equal Suffrage in the Senate.

ARTICLE VI

All Debts contracted and Engagements entered into, before the Adoption of this Constitution, shall be as valid against the United States under this Constitution, as under the Confederation.

This Constitution, and the Laws of the United States which shall be made in Pursuance thereof; and all Treaties made, or which shall be made, under the Authority of the United States, shall be the supreme Law of the Land; and the Judges in every State shall be bound thereby, any Thing in the Constitution or Laws of any State to the Contrary notwithstanding.

The Senators and Representatives before mentioned, and the Members of the several State Legislatures, and all executive and judicial Officers, both of the United States and of the several States, shall be bound by Oath or Affirmation, to support this Constitution; but no religious Test shall ever be required as a Qualification to any Office or public Trust under the United States.

ARTICLE VII

The Ratification of the Conventions of nine States, shall be sufficient for the Establishment of this Constitution between the States so ratifying the Same.

AMENDMENT I

Congress shall make no law respecting an establishment of religion, or prohibiting the free exercise thereof; or abridging the freedom of speech, or of the press; or the right of the people peaceably to assemble, and to petition the Government for a redress of grievances.

AMENDMENT II

A well regulated Militia, being necessary to the security of a free State, the right of the people to keep and bear Arms, shall not be infringed.

AMENDMENT III

No Soldier shall, in time of peace be quartered in any house, without the consent of the Owner, nor in time of war, but in a manner to be prescribed by law.

AMENDMENT IV

The right of the people to be secure in their persons, houses, papers, and effects, against unreasonable searches and seizures, shall not be violated, and no Warrants shall issue, but upon probable cause, supported by Oath or affirmation, and particularly describing the place to be searched, and the persons or things to be seized.

AMENDMENT V

No person shall be held to answer for a capital, or otherwise infamous crime, unless on a presentment or indictment of a Grand Jury, except in cases arising in the land or naval forces, or in the Militia, when in actual service in time of War or public danger; nor shall any person be subject for the same offence to be twice put in jeopardy of life or limb; nor shall be compelled in any criminal case to be a witness against himself, nor be deprived of life, liberty, or property, without due process of law; nor shall private property be taken for public use, without just compensation.

AMENDMENT VI

In all criminal prosecutions, the accused shall enjoy the right to a speedy and public trial, by an impartial jury of the State and district wherein the crime shall have been committed, which district shall have been previously ascertained by law, and to be informed of the nature and cause of the accusation; to be confronted with the witnesses against him; to have compulsory process for obtaining witnesses in his favor, and to have the Assistance of Counsel for his defence.

AMENDMENT VII

In suits at common law, where the value in controversy shall exceed twenty dollars, the right of trial by jury shall be preserved, and no fact tried by a jury, shall be otherwise reexamined in any Court of the United States, than according to the rules of the common law.

AMENDMENT VIII

Excessive bail shall not be required, nor excessive fines imposed, nor cruel and unusual punishments inflicted.

AMENDMENT IX

The enumeration in the Constitution, of certain rights, shall not be construed to deny or disparage others retained by the people.

THE CONSTITUTION OF THE UNITED STATES

AMENDMENT X

The powers not delegated to the United States by the Constitution, nor prohibited by it to the States, are reserved to the States respectively, or to the people.

AMENDMENT XI

The Judicial power of the United States shall not be construed to extend to any suit in law or equity, commenced or prosecuted against one of the United States by Citizens of another State, or by Citizens or Subjects of any Foreign State.

AMENDMENT XII

The Electors shall meet in their respective states and vote by ballot for President and Vice-President, one of whom, at least, shall not be an inhabitant of the same state with themselves; they shall name in their ballots the person voted for as President, and in distinct ballots the person voted for as Vice-President, and they shall make distinct lists of all persons voted for as President, and of all persons voted for as Vice-President, and of the number of votes for each, which lists they shall sign and certify, and transmit sealed to the seat of the government of the United States, directed to the President of the Senate;—the President of the Senate shall, in the presence of the Senate and House of Representatives, open all the certificates and the votes shall then be counted;— The person having the greatest number of votes for President, shall be the President, if such number be a majority of the whole number of Electors appointed; and if no person have such majority, then from the persons having the highest numbers not exceeding three on the list of those voted for as President, the House of Representatives shall choose immediately, by ballot, the President. But in choosing the President, the votes shall be taken by states, the representation from each state having one vote; a quorum for this purpose shall consist of a member or members from two-thirds of the states, and a majority of all the states shall be necessary to a choice. And if the House of Representatives shall not choose a President whenever the right of choice shall devolve upon them, before the fourth day of March next following, then the Vice-President shall act as President, as in case of the death or other constitutional disability of the President.— The person having the greatest number of votes as Vice-President, shall be the Vice-President, if such number be a majority of the whole number of Electors appointed, and if no person have a majority, then from the two highest numbers on the list, the Senate shall choose the Vice-President; a quorum for the purpose shall consist of two-thirds of the whole number of Senators, and a majority of the whole number shall be necessary to a choice. But no person constitutionally ineligible to the office of President shall be eligible to that of Vice-President of the United States.

AMENDMENT XIII

Section 1. Neither slavery nor involuntary servitude, except as a punishment for crime whereof the party shall have been duly convicted, shall exist within the United States, or any place subject to their jurisdiction.

Section 2. Congress shall have power to enforce this article by appropriate legislation.

AMENDMENT XIV

Section 1. All persons born or naturalized in the United States, and subject to the jurisdiction thereof, are citizens of the United States and of the State wherein they reside. No State shall make or enforce any law which shall abridge the privileges or immunities of citizens of the United States; nor shall any State deprive any person of life, liberty, or property, without due process of law; nor deny to any person within its jurisdiction the equal protection of the laws.

Section 2. Representatives shall be apportioned among the several States according to their respective numbers, counting the whole number of persons in each State, excluding Indians not taxed. But when the right to vote at any election for the choice of electors for President and Vice-President of the United States, Representatives in Congress, the Executive and Judicial officers of a State, or the members of the Legislature thereof, is denied to any of the male inhabitants of such State, being twenty-one years of age, and citizens of the United States, or in any way abridged, except for participation in rebellion, or other crime, the basis of representation therein shall be reduced in the proportion which the number of such male citizens shall bear to the whole number of male citizens twenty-one years of age in such State.

Section 3. No person shall be a Senator or Representative in Congress, or elector of President and Vice-President, or hold any office, civil or military, under the United States, or under any State, who, having previously taken an oath, as a member of Congress, or as an officer of the United States, or as a member of any State legislature, or as an executive or judicial officer of any State, to support the Constitution of the United States, shall have engaged in insurrection or rebellion against the same, or given aid or comfort to the enemies thereof. But Congress may by a vote of two-thirds of each House, remove such disability.

Section 4. The validity of the public debt of the United States, authorized by law, including debts incurred for payment of pensions and bounties for services in suppressing insurrection or rebellion, shall not be questioned. But neither the United States nor any State shall assume or pay any debt or obligation incurred in aid of insurrection or rebellion against the United States, or any claim for the loss or emancipation of any slave; but all such debts, obligations and claims shall be held illegal and void.

Section 5. The Congress shall have the power to enforce, by appropriate legislation, the provisions of this article.

AMENDMENT XV

Section 1. The right of citizens of the United States to vote shall not be denied or abridged by the United States or by any State on account of race, color, or previous condition of servitude—

Section 2. The Congress shall have the power to enforce this article by appropriate legislation.

AMENDMENT XVI

The Congress shall have power to lay and collect taxes on incomes, from whatever source derived, without apportionment among the several States, and without regard to any census or enumeration.

AMENDMENT XVII

The Senate of the United States shall be composed of two Senators from each State, elected by the people thereof, for six years; and each Senator shall have one vote. The electors in each State shall have the qualifications requisite for electors of the most numerous branch of the State legislatures.

When vacancies happen in the representation of any State in the Senate, the executive authority of such State shall issue writs of election to fill such vacancies: *Provided,* That the legislature of any State may empower the executive thereof to make temporary appointments until the people fill the vacancies by election as the legislature may direct.

This amendment shall not be so construed as to affect the election or term of any Senator chosen before it becomes valid as part of the Constitution.

AMENDMENT XVIII

Section 1. After one year from the ratification of this article the manufacture, sale, or transportation of intoxicating liquors within, the importation thereof into, or the exportation thereof from the United States and all territory subject to the jurisdiction thereof for beverage purposes is hereby prohibited.

Section 2. The Congress and the several States shall have concurrent power to enforce this article by appropriate legislation.

Section 3. This article shall be inoperative unless it shall have been ratified as an amendment to the Constitution by the legislatures of the several States, as provided in the

Constitution, within seven years from the date of the submission hereof to the States by the Congress.

AMENDMENT XIX

The right of citizens of the United States to vote shall not be denied or abridged by the United States or by any State on account of sex.

Congress shall have power to enforce this article by appropriate legislation.

AMENDMENT XX

Section 1. The terms of the President and the Vice President shall end at noon on the 20th day of January, and the terms of Senators and Representatives at noon on the 3d day of January, of the years in which such terms would have ended if this article had not been ratified; and the terms of their successors shall then begin.

Section 2. The Congress shall assemble at least once in every year, and such meeting shall begin at noon on the 3d day of January, unless they shall by law appoint a different day.

Section 3. If, at the time fixed for the beginning of the term of the President, the President elect shall have died, the Vice President elect shall become President. If a President shall not have been chosen before the time fixed for the beginning of his term, or if the President elect shall have failed to qualify, then the Vice President elect shall act as President until a President shall have qualified; and the Congress may by law provide for the case wherein neither a President elect nor a Vice President shall have qualified, declaring who shall then act as President, or the manner in which one who is to act shall be selected, and such person shall act accordingly until a President or Vice President shall have qualified.

Section 4. The Congress may by law provide for the case of the death of any of the persons from whom the House of Representatives may choose a President whenever the right of choice shall have devolved upon them, and for the case of the death of any of the persons from whom the Senate may choose a Vice President whenever the right of choice shall have devolved upon them.

Section 5. Sections 1 and 2 shall take effect on the 15th day of October following the ratification of this article.

Section 6. This article shall be inoperative unless it shall have been ratified as an amendment to the Constitution by the legislatures of three-fourths of the several States within seven years from the date of its submission.

AMENDMENT XXI

Section 1. The eighteenth article of amendment to the Constitution of the United States is hereby repealed.

Section 2. The transportation or importation into any State, Territory, or possession of the United States for delivery or use therein of intoxicating liquors, in violation of the laws thereof, is hereby prohibited.

Section 3. This article shall be inoperative unless it shall have been ratified as an amendment to the Constitution by conventions in the several States, as provided in the Constitution, within seven years from the date of the submission hereof to the States by the Congress.

AMENDMENT XXII

Section 1. No person shall be elected to the office of the President more than twice, and no person who has held the office of President, or acted as President, for more than two years of a term to which some other person was elected President shall be elected to the office of President more than once. But this Article shall not apply to any person holding the office of President when this Article was proposed by Congress, and shall not prevent any person who may be holding the office of President, or acting as President, during the term within which this Article becomes operative from holding the office of President or acting as President during the remainder of such term.

Section 2. This article shall be inoperative unless it shall have been ratified as an amendment to the Constitution by the legislatures of three-fourths of the several States within seven years from the date of its submission to the States by the Congress.

AMENDMENT XXIII

Section 1. The District constituting the seat of Government of the United States shall appoint in such manner as Congress may direct:

A number of electors of President and Vice President equal to the whole number of Senators and Representatives in Congress to which the District would be entitled if it were a State, but in no event more than the least populous State; they shall be in addition to those appointed by the States, but they shall be considered, for the purposes of the election of President and Vice President, to be electors appointed by a State; and they shall meet in the District and perform such duties as provided by the twelfth article of amendment.

Section 2. The Congress shall have power to enforce this article by appropriate legislation.

AMENDMENT XXIV

Section 1. The right of citizens of the United States to vote in any primary or other election for President or Vice President, for electors for President or Vice President, or for Senator or Representative in Congress, shall not be denied or abridged by the United States or any State by reason of failure to pay poll tax or other tax.

Section 2. The Congress shall have power to enforce this article by appropriate legislation.

AMENDMENT XXV

Section 1. In case of the removal of the President from office or of his death or resignation, the Vice President shall become President.

Section 2. Whenever there is a vacancy in the office of the Vice President, the President shall nominate a Vice President who shall take office upon confirmation by a majority vote of both Houses of Congress.

Section 3. Whenever the President transmits to the President pro tempore of the Senate and the Speaker of the House of Representatives his written declaration that he is unable to discharge the powers and duties of his office, and until he transmits to them a written declaration to the contrary, such powers and duties shall be discharged by the Vice President as Acting President.

Section 4. Whenever the Vice President and a majority of either the principal officers of the executive departments or of such other body as Congress may by law provide, transmit to the President pro tempore of the Senate and the Speaker of the House of Representatives their written declaration that the President is unable to discharge the powers and duties of his office, the Vice President shall immediately assume the powers and duties of the office as Acting President.

Thereafter, when the President transmits to the President pro tempore of the Senate and the Speaker of the House of Representatives his written declaration that no inability exists, he shall resume the powers and duties of his office unless the Vice President and a majority of either the principal officers of the executive department or of such other body as Congress may by law provide, transmit within four days to the President pro tempore of the Senate and the Speaker of the House of Representatives their written declaration that the President is unable to discharge the powers and duties of his office. Thereupon Congress shall decide the issue, assembling within forty-eight hours for that purpose if not in session. If the Congress, within twenty-one days after receipt of the latter written declaration, or, if Congress is not in session, within twenty-one days after Congress is required to assemble, determines by two-thirds vote of both Houses that the President is unable to discharge the powers and duties of his office, the Vice President shall continue to discharge the same as Acting President; otherwise, the President shall resume the powers and duties of his office.

AMENDMENT XXVI

Section 1. The right of citizens of the United States, who are eighteen years of age or older, to vote shall not be denied or abridged by the United States or by any State on account of age.

Section 2. The Congress shall have power to enforce this article by appropriate legislation.

AMENDMENT XXVII

No law, varying the compensation for the services of the Senators and Representatives, shall take effect, until an election of representatives shall have intervened.

NOTES

Chapter 1: Our Guide to Freedom

1. Thomas Jefferson, "First Inaugural Address in Washington, D.C.," *Inaugural Addresses of the Presidents of the United States* (Washington, DC: U.S. G.P.O., 1989), www.bartleby.com/124/pres16.html.
2. James Madison, *The Federalist Papers*, Federalist No. 57, February 19, 1788.
3. Andrew Jackson, "Farewell Address, March 4, 1837," The American Presidency Project, www.presidency.ucsb.edu/ws/?pid=67087.
4. Thomas Jefferson, "A Bill for the More General Diffusion of Knowledge," June 18, 1778.
5. John Adams, "A Dissertation on Canon and Feudal Law, 1765," 7, The Federalist Papers Project, http://thefeder alistpapers.integratedmarket.netdna-cdn.com/wp-content/uploads/2013/01/John-Adams-A-Dissertation-on-Canon-and-Feudal-Law.pdf.
6. Thomas Jefferson, "Letter to Colonel Charles Yancey, January 6, 1816," www.bartleby.com/73/492.html.

Chapter 2: History of the Constitution

1. David O. Stewart, *The Summer of 1787* (New York: Simon & Schuster, 2007), 20.
2. Ibid.
3. "Wednesday, February 21, 1787," *Journals of the Continental Congress, 1774–1789*, ed. Worthington C. Ford et al. (Washington, DC,

1904–37), 32:74, http://memory.loc.gov/cgi-bin/ampage?collId =lljc&fileName=032/lljc032.db&recNum=83.

4. National Archives, "America's Founding Fathers: Delegates to the Constitutional Convention," www.archives.gov/exhibits/ charters/constitution_founding_fathers.html.

5. Biographical sources for the founding fathers in chapter 1: Ibid.; National Constitution Center, "Founding Fathers," http://consti tutioncenter.org/learn/educational-resources/founding-fathers/; Bio, "Founding Fathers," www.biography.com/people/groups/ founding-fathers; Gordon Lloyd, "The Constitutional Conven- tion: Individual Biographies of the Delegates to the Constitu- tional Convention," TeachingAmericanHistory.org, http:// teachingamericanhistory.org/convention/delegates/; Univer- sity of Gronigen, "American History from Revolution to Recon- struction and Beyond: Biographies," 2012, www.let.rug.nl/usa/ biographies/.

6. TeachingAmericanHistory.org, "Alexander Hamilton," http:// teachingamericanhistory.org/static/convention/delegates/ hamilton.html.

Chapter 3: We the People

1. John Adams, "Notes for an Oration at Braintree, Spring 1772," Founders Online, http://founders.archives.gov/documents/ Adams/01-02-02-0002-0002-0001.

2. Deena Winter, "Nebraska School Suggests Teachers Avoid Call- ing Students Boys or Girls to Be 'Gender Inclusive,'" Nebras kaWatchdog.org, Oct. 2, 2014, http://watchdog.org/174768/ gender-inclusive/.

3. Ayn Rand, *Philosophy: Who Needs It* (New York: Signet, 1984).

4. Ronald Reagan, "The Problem of Government, First Address as Governor of California," January 5, 1967, *The Greatest Speeches of Ronald Reagan* (West Palm Beach, FL: NewsMax, 2001), 7.

5. *Respectfully Quoted: A Dictionary of Quotations* (Washington, DC: Library of Congress, 1989), 1593, www.bartleby.com/73/.

Chapter 4: In Order to Form a More Perfect Union

1. Thomas Jefferson, "Letter to Samuel Kercheval, June 12, 1816," TeachingAmericanHistory.org, http://teachingamericanhistory .org/library/document/letter-to-samuel-kercheval/.

Chapter 6: Provide for the Common Defense

1. James Madison, "The Federalist Number 10, 22 November 1787," Founders Online, http://founders.archives.gov/?q=enlightened% 20statesmen%20will%20not%20always%20be%20at%20the% 20helm&s=1111311111&sa=&r=3&sr=.
2. Paul Leicester Ford, "Pamphlets on the Constitution of the United States, Published During Its Discussion by the People, 1787–1788," (Brooklyn, NY, 1888), http://archive.org/details/ cu31924020874099; https://ia600508.us.archive.org/8/items/ cu31924020874099/cu31924020874099.pdf.
3. Thomas Jefferson quoting *Essay on Crimes and Punishments* by Cesare Beccaria, www.monticello.org/site/jefferson/laws-forbid -carrying-armsquotation.
4. George Washington, "Inaugural Address of 1789," National Archives and Records Administration, April 30, 1789, www .archives.gov/exhibits/american_originals/inaugtxt.html.
5. C. S. Lewis, *God in the Dock*, 324.
6. Daniel Webster and Callie L. Bonney, *The Wisdom and Eloquence of Daniel Webster* (New York: John B. Alden, 1886), 62–63.
7. Lyman C. Draper, *Annual Report on the Condition and Improvement of the Common Schools and Education Interests* (Wisconsin: Atwood & Rublee, 1858), 200.

Chapter 7: Promote the General Welfare

1. Patrick Henry, "Give Me Liberty or Give Me Death, March 23, 1775," The Avalon Project, Yale Lillian Goldman Law Library, http://avalon.law.yale.edu/18th_century/patrick.asp.

2. "Dwight D. Eisenhower Quotes," Dwight D. Eisenhower Presidential Library, www.eisenhower.archives.gov/all_about_ike/quotes.html.

Chapter 8: Secure the Blessings of Liberty to Ourselves and Our Posterity

1. "Thomas Jefferson Quotations [see #3]," The Jefferson Monticello, Monticello.org, http://www.monticello.org/site/research-and-collections/chain-email-10-jefferson-quotations#footnote2_8k5i6pd.
2. See www.usdebtclock.org for most current data.
3. "Historical Debt Outstanding—Annual 2000–2014," Treasury Direct, www.treasurydirect.gov/govt/reports/pd/histdebt/histdebt_histo5.htm.
4. "How Much Did the National Debt Increase in 2013?" Bankrupting America, January 2, 2014, www.bankruptingamerica.org/how-much-did-the-national-debt-increase-in-2013-breaking-it-down/#.VV1t1Ov2HwM.
5. "Sep. 10, This Day in History: Nathan Hale volunteers to Spy Behind British Lines," History.com, www.history.com/this-day-in-history/nathan-hale-volunteers-to-spy-behind-british-lines.

Chapter 9: Article 1, the Legislative Branch

1. Introduction by Roger A. Bruns to *A More Perfect Union: The Creation of the United States Constitution* (Washington, DC: National Archives and Records Administration, National Archives Trust Fund Board, 1986), www.archives.gov/exhibits/charters/constitution_history.html.
2. Michael B. Rappaport, "Presentment Clause," *The Heritage Guide to the Constitution, Lesson 8: Lawmaking and the Rule of Law,* The Heritage Foundation, 158, www.heritage.org/constitution/content/pdf/lesson-8.pdf.

NOTES

Chapter 10: Article 2, the Executive Branch

1. Julie Percha, "The 3 Most Contentious Confirmation Hearings," *Washington Post,* February 4, 2015, www.washingtonpost.com/ blogs/the-fix/wp/2015/02/04/the-3-most-contentious -confirmation-hearings-caught-on-tape/.
2. John Adams, "To the Officers of the First Brigade of the Third Division of the Militia of Massachusetts, 11 October 1798," *The Works of John Adams,* vol. 9 *(Letters and State Papers 1799–1811)* (Boston: Little, Brown and Co., 1856), http://oll.libertyfund.org/ titles/adams-the-works-of-john-adams-vol-9-letters-and-state -papers-1799-1811/simple#lf1431-09_head_222.

Chapter 12: Articles 4–7

1. Rich Tucker, "America's Debt, Through the Eyes of the Found- ers," The Heritage Foundation, October 8, 2013, www.heritage .org/research/reports/2013/10/national-debt-and-the-founding -fathers; "About Alexander Hamilton," U.S. Department of the Treasury, November 11, 2010, www.treasury.gov/about/history/ pages/ahamilton.aspx.
2. National Archives, "The Ratification of the Constitution," www .archives.gov/education/lessons/constitution-day/ratification.html.
3. National Archives, "Teaching with Documents: Observing Con- stitution Day," www.archives.gov/education/lessons/constitu tion-day/signers.html.

Chapter 13: The Bill of Rights

1. Mary Beth Marklein, "On Campus: Free Speech for You but Not for Me?" *USA Today,* November 3, 2003, http://usatoday30.usato day.com/news/washington/2003-11-02-free-speech-cover_x.htm; Dr. Susan Berry, "Brandeis Student Journalist: 'Selective Out- rage' on Campus, Students 'Intimidated,' 'Shamed into Silence,'" Breitbart.com, January 11, 2015, http://www.breitbart.com/ big-government/2015/01/11/brandeis-student-journalist

-selective-outrage-on-campus-students-intimidated-shamed
-into-silence/; Kirsten Powers, "How Liberals Ruined College,"
The Daily Beast, May 11, 2015, http://www.thedailybeast.com/
articles/2015/05/11/how-liberals-have-ruined-college.html;
Napp Nazworth, "The Top 10 Worst Offenders of Free Speech on
College Campuses," *Christian Post,* March 6, 2015, http://m.chris
tianpost.com/news/top-10-worst-offenders-of-free
-speech-on-college-campuses-135274/.

Chapter 14: Later Amendments

1. "Amendment XXII: Two-Term Limit on Presidency," Annenberg
    Classroom Interpretation, National Constitution Center, http://
    constitutioncenter.org/constitution/the-amendments/
    amendment-22-presidential-term-limits.

Chapter 15: A Call to Action

1. Andrew A. Lipscomb and Albert Ellery Bergh, eds., "Thomas
    Jefferson, Resolutions Relative to the Alien and Sedition Acts,"
    The Writings of Thomas Jefferson (Washington, DC: Thomas Jeffer-
    son Memorial Association, 1905), http://press-pubs.uchicago
    .edu/founders/documents/v1ch8s41.html.
2. John Adams, *The Political Writings of John Adams,* George W.
    Carey, ed. (Washington, DC: Regnery Publishing Inc., 2000), 157.
3. William J. Bennett, *The Spirit of America* (New York: Simon &
    Schuster, 1997), p. 37.

INDEX

INDEX

INDEX

INDEX

INDEX

presidential pardons, 133
presidential succession, 131–32, 187
presidential veto, 111
president pro tempore, 106, 131,
  223, 224
privacy
  Fourth Amendment, 65,
  162–64, 213
  security vs., 64–65, 162–63
private charity, 75–78
privileges clause, 174–75
Prohibition, 180, 181–82
property rights, 165, 214
proportional income-tax system,
  72–73
protecting innocent life, 89–92

Rand, Ayn, 36
ratification (Article VII), 154–55, 212
Read, George, 13
Reagan, Ronald, 38
recapitulation, 168
Reid, Harry, 110
religion (religious liberty)
  First Amendment, 156–60, 213
  role at Constitutional Convention, 14
  separation of church and state,
  154, 157
residency requirements, 148–49, 185
rights, exercising power by knowing
  your, 30–31
right to bear arms, 60–61, 160–61
Roe v. Wade, 91
Roosevelt, Franklin Delano, 133, 183
"royalty," limits on, 123
Rush, Benjamin, 18

salaries
  of congressmen, 110, 189–90
  of judicial officials, 142
  of the president, 132
searches and seizures, 65, 162–64
Second Amendment, 56–57, 60–61,
  62, 63, 160–61, 213

"secure the blessings of Liberty to
  ourselves and our Posterity,"
  83–93
segregation, 50–51
self-incrimination, 165
self-representation, 166
self-sufficiency, 74, 76–77, 87
Senate, U.S., 104–7
  congressional order, 108–10
  congressional sessions, 108
  limits on power, 120–23
  passing bills, 110–11
  specific powers, 112–20
Senate Journal, 109
separation of church and state,
  154, 157
  Fourteenth Amendment, 217–18
separation of powers, 95, 110–11, 120,
  126
September 11 attacks (2001), 118
Seventh Amendment, 166–67, 214
Seventeenth Amendment, 105,
  179–80, 219
sex slavery, 173
Sherman, Roger, 15
Sixth Amendment, 165–66, 214
Sixteenth Amendment, 178–79, 218
slaves and slavery, 50, 53, 102,
  120–21, 149, 173, 174–76, 177–78
soldiers
  at Constitutional Convention, 17
  quartering of (Third Amendment),
  161–62, 213
  rules of ethical warfare, 59–60
sovereignty of the Constitution
  (Article VI), 152–54, 212
Speaker of the House, 103, 131, 223, 224
speaking up, exercising power by,
  34–38
special-interest groups, 68–69
special sessions, 108, 138
speedy trials, 165–66
state elections, 148–49
state militias, 119
  Second Amendment, 60–61, 160–61
State of the Union address, 137–38

INDEX